3 IN 1

EFFECTIVE COMMUNICATION

115 TECHNIQUES TO CONNECT WITH PEOPLE BY MASTERING THE POWER OF WORDS

BONUS INSIDE

BUILD BETTER RELATIONSHIPS BY CONVEYING YOUR MESSAGE WITH SKILL, CLARITY, AND ELOQUENCE

EMMA LEIGH WEBER

Table of Contents

Introduction

Everyone has experienced the frustration of being misunderstood or feeling disconnected from others, personally and professionally. It can be disheartening when you fail to connect, especially knowing you have something valuable to share. *But what if you could transform your communication abilities, break through these barriers, and effectively express yourself to others?* Imagine the possibilities that would expand for you in your career, relationships, and personal growth.

As an introvert who also struggles with ADHD, I know firsthand the obstacles that can hinder meaningful communication. These challenges sparked a curiosity to delve into communication, relationships, and psychology books. With every page turned are discoveries of new concepts, techniques, and strategies that shed light on the intricate workings of human relationships. Such pearls of wisdom transformed my ability to connect with others and ignited a passion to share this wisdom with the world. And so, this book was born—a culmination of my experiences, extensive research, and profound insights into effective communication, which unlocks the doors to understanding, collaboration, and personal growth.

The book is divided into three major parts, each focused on a key aspect of effective communication: *influence, being interesting,* and *storytelling*. In the section on influence, learn how to understand influence to start integrating it into your communication. With that, discover the techniques and strategies to overcome resistance and objections as you practice your influential muscles.

In the second section, you will focus on becoming more interesting and engaging in your conversations. Master your social skills and get familiar and intimate with social cues. To cap it up, this book further helps you cultivate authenticity in your interactions to build genuine connections that leave a lasting impression.

The last section will unlock the transformative power of narratives, getting to know their benefits and the different types you can add to your conversation arsenal. Discover how to handle resistance and skepticism and avoid storytelling pitfalls and mistakes. Finally, learn to craft compelling stories that inspire, engage, and connect with others on a deeper level.

Throughout this book, there are 39 techniques, tips, and strategies on how to become a more effective communicator. It is intentionally designed this way to serve as your guide along each step of the process. Use it as your guide to navigate the nuances of influence, persuasion, social skills, and storytelling to learn how to communicate with intention and authenticity.

Book 1
The Art of Influential Mindset

Harnessing the Power of Persuasion for Success and Impact

Table of Contents

Chapter 1

Understanding Influence

Influence is the ability to have an impact on the thoughts, actions, and behaviors of others. It involves skillful communication, persuasion, and interpersonal dynamics to shape opinions, inspire action, and create change without exerting control or manipulation but rather about building trust, establishing credibility, and appealing to the emotions and values of others. It operates through communication, persuasion techniques, role modeling, or subtle cues.

The goal of influence can range from inspiring positive change, shaping opinions, driving behaviors, or gaining support for a particular idea or cause. It can motivate others to act, build relationships, and achieve goals. It can also be used to change the way people think about a particular issue. There are different ways to influence others. Some people are naturally persuasive, while others must work harder. However, everyone can learn a few key skills to become more influential.

Social influence theory has been shaped by the contributions of several prominent psychologists who developed key theories in this area. One influential figure is Solomon Asch, who conducted pioneering research on conformity in the 1950s. Asch's experiments involved participants making judgments about the length of lines in the presence of Confederates who provided incorrect answers. His findings demonstrated the powerful impact of social pressure on individual judgment.

Another notable psychologist is Stanley Milgram, known for his controversial Milgram Experiment in the 1960s. Milgram's research investigated obedience to authority by examining participants' willingness to administer electric shocks to others. The study revealed the potential for individuals to engage in harmful actions under the influence of perceived authority figures.

Robert Cialdini is another important figure in the field, known for his work on the principles of persuasion. Cialdini identified six key principles of effective persuasion: *reciprocity, scarcity, authority, consistency, liking,* and *social proof.* His research involved extensive observation of real-world situations and analysis of successful persuasive tactics.

These psychologists developed their theories through rigorous experimentation, data analysis, and observation of human behavior. They systematically designed experiments to study the underlying mechanisms of social influence, observed patterns and effects, and drew conclusions based on their findings. The theories they developed have since provided a foundation for understanding the influence processes and have been widely utilized in effective communication.

Social psychologists and communication scholars have developed several key theories of influence. These theories provide valuable insights into the psychological and social dynamics that shape human behavior and decision-making.

Three prominent theories include the following:

Social Influence Theory

Social influence theory, also known as ***conformity theory***, is a branch of social psychology that explores how the actions, beliefs, and opinions of others influence individuals. It examines how people are persuaded, conform to group norms, and make decisions based on social interactions. In the context of effective communication, understanding social influence theory sheds light on the factors that shape human behavior and decision-making. With this knowledge, communicators can strategically employ persuasive techniques to influence and engage their audience, enhancing the effectiveness of their communication efforts.

Six Key Principles

The principles of social influence provide insights into the underlying mechanisms and factors influencing human behavior in social situations. Below are six key principles of social influence, according to Robert Cialdini.

- **Reciprocity**: The principle of reciprocity suggests that people feel obligated to repay others for favors, gifts, or acts of kindness. When someone does something for you, you often feel a sense of indebtedness and are more likely to comply with their requests or expectations. Reciprocity is often utilized in marketing and sales strategies, where companies offer free samples or small gifts to trigger a sense of reciprocity and increase the likelihood of a purchase.

- **Authority**: The principle of authority suggests that people comply with requests or instructions from individuals perceived as authoritative figures. Authority can be derived from expertise, status, or credentials. People are more likely to follow the recommendations or orders of doctors, professors, or recognized experts in a particular field. The Milgram experiment, which examined obedience to authority, demonstrated the powerful influence authority figures can have on behavior.

- **Social Proof**: The principle of social proof suggests that people look to others for cues on how to behave, especially in situations where they feel uncertain or ambiguous. When you observe others engaging in a particular behavior or holding a certain belief, you conform and adopt similar behaviors or beliefs. Such a principle explains herd mentality, where individuals align their actions with the perceived majority.

- **Consistency**: The principle of consistency suggests that people have a strong desire to act consistently with their previous commitments, beliefs, or statements. Once you make a public commitment or take a stand on a particular issue, you will likely remain consistent. Consistency can be seen in influence techniques that involve obtaining small initial commitments, leading to larger and more significant commitments over time.

- **Liking**: The principle of liking suggests that people are more likely to comply with requests or be influenced by individuals they like or find attractive. Factors such as physical attractiveness, similarity, and praise can contribute to the likability of a person. Influencers and salespeople often try to establish rapport, build relationships, and create a sense of liking to increase their persuasive power.

- **Scarcity**: The principle of scarcity suggests that people perceive items or opportunities as more valuable when they are limited or scarce. The fear of missing out or the desire to possess something unique drives individuals to comply with requests or take advantage of limited-time offers. Marketing and sales strategies employ scarcity, where limited stock, exclusive deals, or time-limited promotions create a sense of urgency and increase the likelihood of action.

These principles provide valuable insights into how individuals can be influenced and applied ethically in various contexts, such as marketing, negotiations, leadership, and social change efforts. However, recognize that social influence can also be used unethically to manipulate or exploit individuals, so employ these principles responsibly and with integrity.

Persuasion Theory

Persuasion theory is a branch of social psychology that explores influencing and changing people's attitudes, beliefs, and behaviors through communication. It involves understanding how messages are crafted, delivered, and received to achieve desired outcomes. These theories provide valuable insights into the mechanisms of persuasion and inform strategies for effective communication by considering factors such as the audience's motivation, ability to process information, and the credibility of the source.

Factors

Persuasion theories examine various factors that influence the effectiveness of persuasive communication, such as:

- **Source of the message**: The source of the message refers to the person or entity delivering the persuasive communication. Factors such as *credibility, expertise, likability,* and *perceived trustworthiness of the source* influence the effectiveness of the message. People are more likely to be persuaded by a source who is perceived as credible, knowledgeable, and trustworthy.

- **Message content**: The content of the message includes the *arguments, evidence, emotional appeals,* and *storytelling techniques* used to convey the intended message. The content should be clear, logical, relevant, and tailored to the audience's needs and values. Strong arguments, supporting evidence, and engaging narratives enhance the persuasiveness of the message.

- **Medium used for communication**: The medium refers to the *channel* or *platform* through which the message is transmitted. Different mediums, such as *face-to-face interactions, written texts, videos*, or *social media,* have different strengths and limitations in reaching and engaging the audience. The choice of the medium should consider the characteristics of the audience, the nature of the message, and the desired outcome. Select a medium that allows for effective message delivery and maximizes the potential for audience engagement.

- **Characteristics of the audience**: The characteristics of the audience, such as *attitudes, beliefs, values, knowledge,* and *demographic factors*, greatly influence the effectiveness of persuasive communication. Audience analysis helps understand the needs, interests, motivations, and potential barriers to persuasion. Tailoring the message to align with the audience's values, addressing their specific concerns, and using language and appeals that resonate with them enhance the persuasive impact of the communication. Consider further factors such as *cognitive abilities, cultural backgrounds,* and *individual differences* within the audience to ensure the message is delivered effectively.

Models of Persuasion

Models of persuasion refer to theoretical frameworks that help explain and understand the process of persuasive communication. These models provide structured guidelines and frameworks for analyzing and predicting how people are influenced by persuasive messages. The key components and processes involved in persuasion, including factors such as the source of the message, message content, communication channels, and characteristics of the audience, were also outlined here.

Models of persuasion, such as the *Elaboration Likelihood Model (ELM)* and the *Theory of Planned Behavior (TPB),* help understand how individuals process and respond to persuasive messages and the factors that influence their attitudes, beliefs, and behaviors.

- **Elaboration Likelihood Model (ELM)**: The ELM proposes two routes of persuasion: *the central route* and *the peripheral route.* The ***central route*** involves careful evaluation and scrutiny of the message content, while the ***peripheral route*** relies on peripheral cues, such as the attractiveness or credibility of the source. ELM further explains when and why different persuasion techniques are more or less effective.

- **Social Judgment Theory (SJT)**: SJT suggests that individuals compare incoming persuasive messages to their existing attitudes or anchor positions. The perceived discrepancy between the message and the individual's attitude determines the level of persuasion. The theory introduces the concepts of latitude of acceptance, latitude of rejection, and latitude of non-commitment to explain the range of possible attitude changes.

- **Theory of Planned Behavior (TPB)**: The TPB helps explain and predict human behavior based on an individual's attitudes, subjective norms, and perceived behavioral control. It says that people's intentions to do something are influenced by their attitudes, what they think others expect of them, and how much control they think they have over the behavior. For example, if you want to convince someone to recycle more, you need to address their beliefs about recycling, what others think about it, and how easy it is for them to recycle. Using the principles of the TPB, you can create persuasive messages that can change people's behavior.

- **Cognitive Dissonance Theory**: Cognitive dissonance theory posits that individuals experience discomfort when their attitudes or beliefs conflict with their behaviors or new information. Persuasion attempts can create cognitive dissonance and offer a solution or alternative that reduces the discomfort. Individuals are likely to change their attitudes or behaviors by reducing dissonance.

Individuals who encounter cognitive dissonance are motivated to reduce the inconsistency between their beliefs and behaviors. Several ways people may attempt to resolve this tension include:

- Changing one of the conflicting beliefs, values, or attitudes.
- Acquiring new information or beliefs to justify the conflicting belief or behavior.
- Rationalizing the conflicting belief or behavior.
- Denial or selective exposure.
- Changing the importance of conflicting beliefs.

Social Identity Theory

Social Identity Theory (SIT) is a theory that explains how individuals' sense of self and identity is shaped by their membership in social groups. Developed by Henri Tajfel and John Turner in the 1970s, SIT provides insights into the intricate interplay between personal and group identity, shedding light on how groups influence individuals and contribute to social behavior. According to this theory, people strive to maintain a positive social identity by emphasizing the positive qualities and distinctiveness of their group compared to other groups.

In the context of effective communication, understanding social identity theory, tailor your messages to appeal to the social identities of your audience. By highlighting shared values, beliefs, and experiences, you can create a sense of belonging and unity, increasing your communication's persuasiveness. Additionally, recognizing the potential influence of social identity can further help you anticipate and address potential resistance or skepticism from individuals who strongly identify with competing groups.

Core Principles

The following compromises SIT:

- **Group Categorization**: SIT posits that individuals naturally categorize themselves and others into social groups based on shared characteristics, such as nationality, ethnicity, religion, or organizational affiliation. Such categorization is the foundation for social identification and shapes attitudes, beliefs, and behaviors.

- **Social Comparison**: Once individuals have identified with a particular group, they use social comparison processes, such as comparing their group to other groups, to establish a positive social identity. Individuals bolster their self-esteem and enhance their sense of belonging by emphasizing their group's positive qualities and achievements.

- **In-Group Bias**: Social Identity Theory suggests that individuals favor their group, known as in-group bias. This bias leads to positive evaluations of the in-group and its members while often fostering negative perceptions of out-group members. In-group bias can contribute to intergroup conflicts, stereotypes, and discrimination.

- **Intergroup Differentiation**: SIT explains how groups differentiate themselves from other groups through accentuation of differences and distinctiveness. By emphasizing unique attributes and values, groups seek to maintain a positive social identity and create boundaries between themselves and other groups.

These theories provide frameworks for understanding the various mechanisms and processes through which influence operates in social interactions and can help explain the dynamics of persuasion, conformity, and group behavior.

Chapter 2

Building Influence

Influential styles determine how you exert influence and persuade others. Different influential styles have varying impacts on the outcomes of communication interactions. Learn to adopt these influential styles in this chapter to tailor your approach to effectively engage and persuade others, leading to more successful and impactful communication outcomes.

Styles

Everyone has their communication styles, but in addition to that, people also have their influential styles. As a communicator, know which one you prefer to determine how you exert influence and persuade others. The choice of influential style depends on the context, the audience, and the desired outcome of the communication.

There are four main influential styles, including:

Logical and Rational Style

The logical style is characterized by its emphasis on logical reasoning and objective information. It excels in presenting clear, structured, and evidence-based arguments. Communicators who employ this style are adept at presenting facts, data, and logical analysis to support their ideas. The organization of thoughts and evidence to form a cohesive narrative was also carefully considered to engage the rational thinking of the audience by appealing to their logic and analytical mindset. Logical communicators also articulate ideas in a logical sequence, making it easier for the audience to follow and comprehend complex information.

A logical and rational style is proven effective when a well-structured and logical approach is required to sway opinions and influence decisions. Those who employ this style highlight the practical benefits and logical consistency of their ideas. Tangible outcomes were focused, solutions aligned with common sense, and rational decision-making were proposed. Showcasing the practicality of arguments increases the likelihood of the audience accepting and acting upon the suggestions.

Emotional and Personal Style

The emotional style of influence is centered around appealing to the personal emotions of the audience to convey a message and elicit a desired response. Such a style recognizes that humans are inherently emotional beings, and their decisions and actions are heavily influenced by how they feel.

Research has consistently shown that emotions play a role in decision-making. When emotions are engaged, they can override logical thinking and shape your perceptions, preferences, and actions.

Those who use the emotional style leverage this understanding to influence the audience's attitudes, behaviors, and beliefs. Feelings such as empathy, joy, fear, or hope were evoked to connect with the audience on a deeper level. By evoking strong emotions, you create a sense of urgency or desire, making your message more memorable and compelling.

Despite the effectiveness of emotional appeals, as a communicator, strike a balance and ensure authenticity. Manipulating emotions for personal gain can undermine your trust and credibility. But with authenticity and sincerity, you build stronger connections and foster trust with your audience.

Cooperative and Collaborative Style

The cooperative style is rooted in collaboration, cooperation, and building positive relationships. Those who adopt this style prioritize the needs and perspectives of others, aiming to find common ground and foster a sense of unity. Communicators using this style understand that effective communication is not about asserting dominance or winning arguments but rather about creating a harmonious environment.

Finding win-win solutions creates outcomes that satisfy the needs and goals of all parties involved, paving the way for sustainable and mutually beneficial results.

Key Elements of Cooperative Style

Building cooperative style are the following elements:

- **Active Listening**: Communicators using the cooperative style actively listen to others, seeking to understand their viewpoints, concerns, and needs. They show genuine interest and empathy, creating a safe and open space for communication.

- **Collaboration and Teamwork**: Cooperative communicators focus on collaboration and teamwork, inviting others to contribute, thereby valuing diverse perspectives. Brainstorming, problem-solving, and finding win-win solutions were also encouraged.

- **Building Trust and Rapport**: Trust and rapport are essential for the cooperative style. Communicators invest time and effort into building relationships, demonstrating respect, and valuing the opinions of others.

- **Seeking Consensus**: Rather than imposing their ideas or decisions, cooperative communicators strive to find consensus. Engaging in dialogue helps them explore different viewpoints and facilitate collective decision-making.

Assertive and Expertise-Based

The assertive and expertise-based influence style is a direct and confident communication approach, combining confidence, knowledge, and authority to persuade others effectively. Communicators who adopt this style assert their ideas, opinions, and recommendations with conviction while providing evidence and expertise to support claims. This confidence helps captivate the attention of others and establishes credibility, making it easier to persuade and influence.

In presenting compelling arguments, thoughts and ideas are presented skillfully. Using this style, leverage your knowledge to position yourself as a reliable and trustworthy source. The assertive and expert-based influence style is especially effective when expertise and credibility are valued, and the goal is to provide accurate information and gain buy-in based on solid evidence.

As you learn more about this style, know you are not steamrolling your audience. Strike a balance between assertiveness and respect for others' viewpoints, fostering a collaborative and open-minded environment for effective communication.

Assessment

Understanding and adapting your preference in a conversation leads to more successful and impactful communication outcomes. To understand your influential style, assess your strengths and areas for improvement by doing the following:

Assess Your Communication Patterns

Pay attention to your typical communication patterns. Reflect on the specific strategies and techniques you tend to use when trying to influence others. *Are you more inclined to present logical arguments, appeal to emotions, build relationships, or assert your thoughts and preferences?* Notice any recurring patterns or tendencies that emerge in your interactions. Consider how you typically build rapport and establish trust with others.

Reflect on Past Experiences

Think about situations where you have successfully influenced others in the past. Recall instances where you persuaded someone to see your point of view or take a specific action. Consider how you approached the communication and what strategies you employed.

Seek Feedback

Ask trusted friends, colleagues, or mentors for their observations and feedback on your communication style. Inquire about how they perceive your approach to influence and persuasion. Insights provide valuable perspectives and shed light on your natural tendencies.

Consider Contextual Factors

Evaluate how your influence style varies across different contexts and audiences. *Are there situations where you naturally adapt your approach?* Notice any shifts in your behavior based on factors such as the nature of the topic, the relationship with the person, or the desired outcome.

Observe Reactions

Pay attention to how others respond to your influence attempts. *Do they seem more receptive to certain strategies? Are there particular approaches that consistently yield positive outcomes?* Notice any patterns in the reactions and responses you receive from different individuals.

Explore Multiple Styles

Familiarize yourself with influential styles, such as logical, emotional, cooperative, or assertive. Study their characteristics, strengths, and potential drawbacks. Assess how well each style aligns with your observations and feedback received.

Reflect on Alignment and Effectiveness

Consider how aligned your dominant influence style is with your values, communication goals, and desired outcomes. Reflect on the effectiveness of your style in achieving positive results and building strong relationships. Identify any areas for growth or opportunities to expand your repertoire.

Remember, influence styles are not fixed or limited to a single approach. Flexibility and adaptability are key to effective communication. As you identify your dominant style, be open to refining and expanding your approach to suit different situations and individuals. With self-awareness and ongoing practice, you can refine your influence style and become a more impactful communicator.

Implementation

Some practical techniques and strategies to implement your brand of influence to communicate effectively.

Establish Rapport

Building rapport is creating a connection with someone else, allowing you to build trust and understanding with the other person.

- **Find common ground;** it could be anything from sharing a hobby to having a similar background.
- **Show genuine interest** in the other person by actively listening to them, asking questions, and providing feedback. Doing so demonstrates that you value their perspective and fosters a deeper connection.
- **Implement positive body language,** including making eye contact, smiling, and nodding. Positive body language shows that you are engaged in the conversation.

Establish Trust

Trust enables open and transparent communication, where individuals feel safe to express their thoughts, feelings, and ideas without fear of judgment or betrayal. It is the confidence and belief that others have in our honesty, reliability, and competence. When trust is present, communication flows more smoothly, misunderstandings are minimized, and collaborative problem-solving becomes possible. Here are some strategies to build trust:

- **Keep your promises and follow through on your commitments.** Your words and actions should be aligned.
- **Communicate honestly and authentically.** Avoid exaggeration or manipulation, as this can damage trust.
- **Keep information that is shared with you confidential.** Keeping a trusted secret to yourself shows that you are trustworthy.

Establish Credibility

Credibility works hand in hand with trust. To effectively influence others, establish trust and credibility by demonstrating expertise, providing evidence, and presenting oneself as knowledgeable and reliable. Building credibility requires presenting well-researched evidence, sharing relevant qualifications, and consistently delivering reliable information. People are more likely to be persuaded by individuals they perceive as credible and trustworthy. To help you establish credibility, do the following:

- **Continuously expand your knowledge and expertise in your field of interest.** Stay updated with the latest research, trends, and developments to provide accurate and relevant information, positioning you as a credible source.

- **Showcase your skills and competence through your work and achievements.** Highlight your accomplishments, certifications, qualifications, and relevant experiences. This evidence of competence enhances your credibility and instills confidence in others.

- **Engage in professional communities, attend industry events, and collaborate with other experts.** By networking and building relationships with credible individuals in your field, you enhance your credibility through association.

First Impressions Matter

Often, first impressions impact how others perceive you and your ability to influence them. It sets the stage for successful communication and influence. Follow the given strategies below to make a good first impression:

- Be hygienic.
- Dressing appropriately for the occasion.
- Making eye contact and smiling.
- Using a clear and concise speaking voice.
- Being polite and respectful.
- Actively listening to the other person.

Know Your Audience

Tailoring your message to resonate with your audience is necessary. Understanding the needs, values, and perspectives of the individuals you are communicating with allows you to frame your message in a way that appeals to their interests and concerns. Adapting your language, tone, and examples to align with your audience's background and preferences increases the likelihood of successfully influencing their thinking.

Appeal to Emotions

Craft your communication to evoke positive emotions, such as joy, hope, or empathy, to engage your audience and elicit a favorable response. Appealing to your audience's emotions creates a deeper connection and increases the impact of your message. However, use emotional appeals ethically and responsibly, ensuring they are aligned with the intended message.

Utilize Social Proof

People often look to others for guidance when making decisions. By leveraging social proof, such as testimonials, case studies, or statistics, you can influence individuals by demonstrating that others have already adopted your viewpoint or have taken your desired action. Highlighting success stories and positive experiences can reassure and build confidence in your message.

Chapter 3

Overcoming Resistance and Objections

When engaging in persuasive communication, it is common to encounter resistance and objections from others. These challenges can hinder the progress of your arguments and make it difficult to influence the beliefs and behaviors of your audience. However, by understanding the nature of resistance and objections and employing effective strategies, you can navigate these roadblocks and increase your chances of successfully persuading them. Under this chapter are a variety of techniques to overcome resistance and objections that you can use in your daily conversations.

Listen Actively

Influence is a two-way process. To address resistance and objections effectively, actively listen and genuinely engage in dialogue with your audience. Acknowledge their viewpoint, validate their concerns, and show genuine interest in their perspective. Listening to the perspectives and concerns of your audience address objections and tailor your arguments accordingly. Demonstrating empathy and understanding further creates a safe space for open dialogue that helps build trust and increases the likelihood of them considering alternative viewpoints.

Anticipate and Prepare

Like the famous Stephen Covey quote, *"Wars are won in the general's tent."* Before you even begin to engage in persuasive communication, take the time to anticipate potential objections and resistance. Make a list, then research and understand the common counterarguments and concerns related to your message. Preparing thoughtful responses in advance helps address objections confidently and provides compelling counterpoints. This demonstrates your expertise and enhances your credibility.

Provide Evidence

When faced with objections, provide evidence and examples to support your position. Use data, research findings, or real-life anecdotes to illustrate the validity of your argument to strengthen your case and counteract any doubts or misconceptions contributing to resistance. Visual aids, such as charts or graphs, can also be impactful in presenting evidence.

Reframe

Resistance and objections often arise from a difference in perspectives or misunderstandings. Reframe your message by finding common ground with your audience to overcome this. Highlight shared goals, values, or interests that align with your argument. By emphasizing these areas of agreement, you create a sense of unity and collaboration, making it easier to address objections constructively.

Be Proactive

Proactively address potential concerns and objections before your audience raises them. Anticipate the doubts or fears that may arise and incorporate them into your persuasive narrative. By acknowledging and addressing these concerns upfront, you demonstrate transparency. It also shows that you have considered multiple viewpoints, which fosters trust and reduces resistance.

Compromise

When objections are rooted in conflicting interests or preferences, seek to compromise by finding win-win solutions. Understand the underlying motivations and needs of your audience and look for opportunities to meet those needs while still advancing your argument. This collaborative approach demonstrates flexibility and a willingness to find common ground, making resistance less likely.

Maintain an Open Mind

While overcoming resistance and objections, maintain a respectful and open-minded attitude. Avoid becoming defensive or dismissive when faced with challenging questions or opposing viewpoints. Instead, engage in respectful dialogue, validate the concerns of your audience, and respond with thoughtful and well-reasoned arguments to foster a constructive atmosphere and increase the chances of successful persuasion.

Book 2
The Art of Intrapersonal Interactions

Creating a Positive and Inclusive Communication Environment

Table of Contents

Chapter 1

Social Skills

Effective communication goes beyond words. It also involves mastering the art of social skills. Social skills navigate social interactions and communicating with others, ranging from abilities such as active listening, empathy, nonverbal communication, and conflict resolution. Honing your social skills creates a positive and inclusive communication environment where your messages are received openly, and your interactions leave a lasting impact. This chapter explores the different components of social skills in communication, understands their significance, and how they contribute to successful interpersonal interactions.

Significance

Well-developed social skills will help you:

- Establish rapport and trust with others.
- Resolve conflicts and manage challenges.
- Create a positive and inclusive environment.
- Express yourself clearly and concisely.
- Work effectively in teams.

- Negotiate effectively.
- Constructively manage your emotions.
- Adapt to different social situations.

Below are some examples of how social skills can be used in different settings:

- In a personal setting:
  - Ask your partner how their day was.
  - Listen to your friend's concerns.
  - Help your child with their homework.

- In a professional setting:
  - Give a presentation to your colleagues.
  - Resolve a conflict with a coworker.
  - Negotiate a contract with a client.

Strategies to Develop Social Skills

When you find social interaction tough, follow these strategies to enhance your social skills:

- **Be aware of your body language,** which can convey much about your feelings, even when you are silent. Strive for an open, inviting posture, avoiding defensive stances like crossed arms or averted gaze.

- **Know your strengths and weaknesses.** *What are you good at in social situations? What could you improve on?* Once you know your strengths and weaknesses, you can develop strategies to improve your weak areas.

- **Remain respectful,** even in disagreement. Refrain from resorting to name-calling, insults, or aggression.

- **Develop empathy.** Strive to understand the other person's perspective and emotions.

- **Assertiveness** allows you to advocate for yourself and your beliefs respectfully, essential for meeting your needs and cultivating healthy relationships.

- As the saying goes, **practice makes perfect**. Frequent interactions with others foster the improvement of social skills. Engage with people as much as possible.

- **Find a socially adept mentor.** Guidance from a professional can facilitate your learning and improvement.

- **Self-educate** by reading books and articles about social skills and consider enrolling in classes focusing on these skills. Many resources and structured learning environments can help you develop and enhance these crucial life skills.

Improving social skills demands patience and diligence, but the outcome is rewarding.

Barriers to Social Skills Development

Several barriers can hinder the development of these essential skills, such as:

Internal Barriers

Internal barriers to social skills development refer to the psychological and emotional obstacles individuals face, which can hinder individuals from engaging in social interactions, expressing themselves authentically, or taking risks to develop their social skills. Overcoming these internal barriers requires self-reflection, building self-confidence, challenging negative self-perceptions, and adopting a growth mindset. Addressing and overcoming these internal barriers can unlock your social potential and develop stronger interpersonal connections. These barriers may include:

- ***Low self-esteem*** refers to having a negative perception of yourself, often accompanied by feelings of inadequacy and self-worth. Such a feeling can hinder the development of social skills, causing you to doubt your abilities, feel unworthy of social connections, or fear rejection.

- ***Self-doubt*** involves a lack of confidence in your abilities, leading to uncertainty and hesitation in social interactions. It can prevent individuals from expressing themselves authentically, taking social risks, or engaging fully in conversations.

- ***Fear of judgment*** is the apprehension or anxiety about being evaluated or criticized by others. It can hinder the development of social skills by causing you to avoid social situations, hold back from expressing opinions, or constantly seek approval, thus limiting your authentic communication.

- ***Perfectionism*** is a tendency to set unrealistic standards for oneself and constantly strive for flawlessness. It can impede the development of social skills by creating a fear of making mistakes, leading to self-consciousness and self-criticism in social interactions.

- ***Limiting beliefs*** are negative beliefs or assumptions you hold about your social abilities. These beliefs may include thinking you are socially awkward, boring, or incapable of building meaningful connections. Such beliefs can hinder the development of social skills by creating a self-fulfilling prophecy and limiting your willingness to engage in social interactions.

To overcome these internal barriers, do the following:

- **Overcoming low self-esteem:** Building self-esteem involves practicing self-care, self-compassion, and positive self-talk. Setting realistic goals, celebrating small achievements, and surrounding yourself with supportive individuals can help boost self-esteem and help you build a positive self-image.

- **Overcoming self-doubt:** Challenging self-doubt involves recognizing and reframing negative thoughts. Engaging in positive self-affirmations, focusing on past successes, and seeking validation from within rather than solely relying on external validation can help you overcome self-doubt and build self-confidence.

- **Overcoming fear of judgment:** Addressing the fear of judgment requires shifting the focus from others' opinions to your values and authenticity. Practicing self-acceptance, embracing vulnerability, and gradually exposing yourself to social situations can help reduce the fear of judgment and increase comfort in expressing yourself authentically.

- **Overcoming perfectionism:** Adopt a growth mindset and accept that making mistakes is a natural part of learning. Setting realistic expectations, celebrating progress rather than demanding perfection, and reframing mistakes as opportunities for growth can help you overcome perfectionism and promote a healthier approach to social interactions.

- **Overcoming limiting beliefs about social abilities:** Challenging limiting beliefs about social abilities requires cognitive restructuring and evidence-based thinking. Actively seeking counter-evidence, focusing on strengths and past positive social experiences, and seeking social support can help you challenge and replace limiting beliefs with more empowering and accurate beliefs about your social abilities.

Cognitive Barriers

Cognitive barriers to social skills development pertain to the thought patterns and cognitive processes that hinder your ability to develop effective social skills. These barriers can include:

- ***Difficulties understanding social cues*** refer to challenges in accurately interpreting nonverbal cues, facial expressions, body language, and tone of voice in social interactions. It can lead to miscommunication, misunderstandings, and difficulty responding appropriately to others' cues.

- ***Misinterpreting others' intentions*** involves attributing incorrect motives or meanings to their words or actions. It can lead to misunderstandings, conflicts, and strained relationships if individuals consistently misinterpret others' intentions as negative or hostile.

- ***Overthinking social interactions*** involves excessively analyzing and replaying past conversations or anticipating future interactions. It can lead to self-consciousness and anxiety, hindering spontaneous communication.

- ***Lacking perspective-taking abilities*** means difficulty understanding or empathizing with others' viewpoints, emotions, or experiences. It can hinder effective communication and lead to misunderstandings or a lack of connection in social interactions.

- ***Cognitive biases*** are mental shortcuts or tendencies that influence our judgment and decision-making. Some examples are assuming negative intent, which refers to the tendency to attribute negative motives to others' actions, and making snap judgments, which involves forming quick, often unconscious opinions about others without sufficient evidence or understanding.

These can all impede social skills development. Overcoming cognitive barriers requires certain actions, such as:

- **Overcoming difficulties in understanding social cues:** Engage in role-playing exercises, watch videos or tutorials on nonverbal communication, and actively practice in social settings to improve understanding of social cues.

- **Overcoming misinterpreting others' intentions:** To overcome this barrier, practice active listening, ask clarifying questions, and avoid jumping to conclusions. Taking the time to understand others' perspectives, giving them the benefit of the doubt, and practicing open-mindedness reduces the tendency to misinterpret intentions.

- **Overcoming overthinking social interactions:** Overcoming overthinking requires shifting focus from excessive self-analysis to being present at the moment.

Practicing mindfulness techniques, reframing negative thoughts, and reminding oneself of past successful social interactions can help alleviate overthinking and promote a more relaxed and authentic communication style.

- **Overcoming lacking perspective-taking abilities:** Building perspective-taking abilities involves practicing empathy, active listening, and understanding others' experiences. Engaging in perspective-taking exercises, actively seeking diverse perspectives, and reflecting on your biases help expand perspective-taking abilities and enhance communication effectiveness.

- **Overcoming cognitive biases, such as assuming negative intent and making snap judgments:** Develop an awareness and conscious effort to challenge automatic thought patterns. Consider alternative explanations, seek evidence before concluding, and practice open-mindedness to counteract these biases and promote fair and accurate judgment in social interactions.

Environmental barriers

Environmental barriers limit access to resources, opportunities, and a sense of belonging. Some common environmental barriers include:

- ***Poor social modeling*** hinders you from forming healthy relationships and connecting with your community. This barrier can be caused by past trauma or challenges that negatively impact your ability to interact with others.

- ***Language barriers*** limit communication and create isolation, especially for individuals new to a country or community.

- ***Cultural differences*** lead to misunderstandings and feelings of exclusion, particularly for individuals who have experienced discrimination or marginalization due to their cultural identity.

- ***Technology barriers*** prevent you from accessing important information or participating in online communities. This barrier disproportionately affects those unfamiliar with technology, such as seniors or people from low-income backgrounds.

- ***Lack of social support*** negatively impacts mental health and well-being, causing feelings of isolation, depression, and anxiety. This barrier is often faced by individuals who have experienced trauma or other challenges that have made it difficult to form healthy relationships and social connections.

Identify and overcome obstacles to break through environmental barriers. Each barrier requires different strategies to overcome it. For instance—

- **Poor social modeling:** Look for positive role models and mentors within your community or even on a larger scale. Engage in support groups, workshops, or classes that help build communication and interpersonal skills.

- **Language barriers:** Utilizing language learning resources, such as classes, apps, or language exchange programs, can help to improve language proficiency. Practice speaking the language in various contexts, and do not be afraid to make mistakes; these are part of the learning process.

- **Cultural difference:** Becoming more aware and understanding of other cultures can help overcome cultural barriers. Participate in cultural exchange programs or initiatives that celebrate diversity. Educate yourself about other cultures through reading, documentaries, or direct conversations with people from different backgrounds.

- **Technology barriers:** Access to digital literacy programs and resources can help those struggling with technology. Public libraries, community centers, and adult education programs often offer free or low-cost training. Online tutorials and help forums can also provide useful guidance.

- **A lack of social support:** Building a strong social network can help to overcome feelings of isolation. Join clubs, volunteer in the community, or participate in online communities centered around shared interests. Professional counseling or therapy can also be beneficial, especially for those dealing with trauma or mental health issues.

Overcoming environmental barriers is a task that requires your initiative and community support. While you make strides by being proactive and utilizing available resources, communities can aid in this process by creating an inclusive environment that celebrates diversity and fosters cross-cultural understanding.

Chapter 2

Social Cues

Social cues are the nonverbal and verbal signals to communicate information in social interactions. Social cues provide valuable information about a person's emotions, attitudes, and intentions, allowing you to understand and interpret their messages beyond their words. Being attuned to social cues enables effective communication by helping you adjust your responses, demonstrate empathy, and establish rapport with others.

In this increasingly complex and interconnected world, reading these cues as they reveal what someone is thinking and feeling is more important than ever. Decoding social cues plays an important role in human interaction. The capacity to interpret social cues holds multiple benefits, such as enabling you to build rapport with others, aiding in resolving conflicts, and helping avoid misunderstandings. It also facilitates better decision-making and assists in effectively navigating social situations.

Types of Social Cues

There are different types of social cues, such as:

Vocal Cues

Vocal cues are elements of speech, such as tone and pitch, that communicate beyond the actual words. A calm tone may suggest confidence, whereas a high-pitched, shaky voice might indicate nervousness.

Facial expressions

Expressions can indicate emotions such as happiness, sadness, anger, surprise, or fear, along with cues about confidence or interest.

Gestures

Body movements like hand gestures, head nods, or body posture can express agreement, disagreement, interest, or disinterest.

Proxemics

Proxemics refers to studying personal space and how individuals use and perceive space in social interactions. It examines the physical distance people maintain between themselves and others and how it affects communication and social dynamics. Some people like to stand close, while others prefer to stay far away.

Proxemics help you navigate these preferences and adjust your behavior accordingly. This cue will ensure that you respect other people's boundaries and create a comfortable environment for effective communication.

Paralinguistic Cues

Non-verbal elements accompanying verbal communication, such as pauses, sighs, laughter, and vocal intonation, can convey additional emotional and attitudinal information.

The brain processes social cues through a network involving various regions. The prefrontal cortex is involved in decision-making and social cognition, the amygdala processes emotional information, and the insula handles bodily sensations, including emotional responses. Research shows that the brain processes social cues quickly, often before conscious awareness, emphasizing their automatic and pre-attentive nature. Understanding the intricacies of social cues and their neural processing can facilitate effective communication and interaction in diverse social contexts.

Challenges

The following are the challenges you may face when trying to decode social cues:

Cultural Differences

Cultural differences make decoding social cues challenging because different cultures have unique norms, values, and expectations regarding nonverbal communication. Gestures, facial expressions, and body language can have varying meanings across cultures, leading to potential misunderstandings. For example, eye contact, personal space, and silence can differ significantly from culture to culture. Without an understanding of these cultural nuances, it can be challenging to interpret and respond to social cues accurately. Developing cultural sensitivity and learning about different cultural norms help navigate these challenges and enhance cross-cultural communication.

Individual Differences

Each person has unique communication styles, preferences, and nonverbal cues. Some individuals may express their emotions subtly, while others may be more expressive. Personal experiences, personality traits, and communication habits can also influence how people convey and interpret social cues. Neurodiversity, cultural background, and social conditioning can further contribute to individual differences in decoding social cues. Being mindful of these variations and engaging in active listening, empathy, and open communication bridge the gap and facilitate a better understanding of the different communication styles between you and others.

Ambiguity

Social cues can also be vague or have multiple interpretations. Sometimes, people may intentionally or unintentionally send mixed signals, making it difficult to decipher their true intentions or emotions. Ambiguous facial expressions, subtle gestures, or ambiguous verbal cues can create confusion and uncertainty in social interactions. The lack of clarity can lead to miscommunication, misunderstandings, and challenges in forming meaningful connections. To navigate ambiguity, make it a point to listen actively. Always ask clarifying questions and look for ways to have open and honest communication. Doing so can help you reduce potential misunderstandings.

Distractions

Distractions divert your attention from the actual social interaction. When distracted by external factors such as noise, visual stimuli, or competing tasks, you may miss important nonverbal cues or fail to engage in the conversation.

Internal factors like preoccupying thoughts or personal concerns can further limit your ability to focus on social cues. Being aware of these distractions is key to addressing them. When you see yourself getting distracted in a conversation, you can consciously listen and return your attention to the present moment.

Personal Biases

While everyone has individual differences, everyone also has personal biases that can influence how social cues are interpreted and perceived. Biases are preconceived notions, stereotypes, or judgments based on your beliefs, experiences, or cultural conditioning. These biases can cloud judgment, leading to misinterpretations or misattributions of others' intentions or emotions. Your biases can cause you to make assumptions, jump to conclusions, or overlook important cues that do not align with your preconceived notions.

Decoding social cues can be difficult. The fact that they are diverse and their interpretation can vary based on context makes it even more challenging. Some individuals might be more adept at decoding these cues due to social experience, sensitivity, or natural aptitude. Despite that, it is a skill that can be learned.

Techniques

In the complex fabric of human communication, the ability to decode social cues is a key thread that weaves our understanding of one another. Developing this skill can lead to more effective communication, deeper connections, and increased empathy. To help you on your journey of self-improvement, here is a comprehensive collection of techniques for enhancing your ability to decode social cues.

Tune into the Subtleties of Tone

The human voice conveys many emotions and attitudes. To improve your ability to decode social cues, practice listening carefully to pitch, volume, and speech rate variations. These nuances can reveal hidden layers of meaning, allowing you to understand the speaker's message better.

Cultivate Empathy and Compassion

Develop empathy by engaging in activities that foster empathy, such as volunteering, reading novels, or conversing with diverse individuals. These experiences can broaden your understanding of the human experience and strengthen your empathic abilities.

Nurture Emotional Intelligence

Emotional intelligence (EQ) helps in navigating the complexities of interpersonal relationships. To develop your EQ, practice self-awareness, self-regulation, and social awareness. Regularly reflect on your emotions and how they influence your behavior to become more attuned to the emotions of others.

Embrace Cultural Diversity

The world is a beautiful mosaic of cultures, each with its norms, customs, and social cues. Invest time learning about different cultural practices and values to communicate effectively across cultures. This knowledge will help you adapt your communication style and better understand the perspectives of those from diverse backgrounds, leading to stronger connections and a deeper appreciation for the richness of human diversity.

Seek Constructive Feedback

Every journey of self-improvement benefits from honest feedback. Ask trusted friends, family members, or colleagues to provide insights into your communication style and social skills. Their feedback can help you identify areas for improvement and develop targeted growth strategies.

Observe and Learn from Expert Communicators

Watch how communicators adapt their communication style to suit the needs of their audience. Analyzing their techniques and strategies can help you improve your communication skills.

Engage in Purposeful Conversations

Seek opportunities to engage in meaningful conversations that challenge your ability to decode social cues to improve your social skills and become more empathetic.

Read Between the Lines

Develop your ability to read between the lines by paying attention to the context of a conversation, the speaker's choice of words, and any non-verbal cues to identify underlying emotions or intentions that may not be explicitly stated.

Expand Your Emotional Vocabulary

Enrich your emotional vocabulary by learning about various emotions and their corresponding expressions to identify and describe the emotions of others more accurately, enhancing your ability to decode social cues.

Pursue Lifelong Learning

Self-improvement is a lifelong journey. Committing to lifelong learning can improve your ability to decode social cues and foster meaningful connections. Continuously seek opportunities to expand your knowledge, develop new skills, and grow as a communicator.

Disabilities Hindering Interpretation of Social Cues

Learning disabilities like dyslexia, dysgraphia, dyscalculia, Auditory Processing Disorder (APD), and Visual Processing Disorder (VPD) affect the interpretation of social cues in various ways:

- **Dyslexia:** Challenges with reading and decoding words hindering understanding written communication, which may include interpreting social cues in texts or emails, affecting social interactions and comprehension.

- **Dysgraphia:** Struggles with forming letters and words can make it difficult to express thoughts clearly in writing, potentially leading to misinterpretations or misunderstandings in social contexts.

- **Dyscalculia:** Difficulties with numbers and math operations can extend to challenges in understanding sequences or patterns in social interactions, possibly affecting the ability to follow social norms or rules.

- **Auditory Processing Disorder (APD):** Trouble processing spoken language impairs the understanding of vocal tones and nuances, essential for interpreting verbal social cues in conversations.

- **Visual Processing Disorder (VPD):** Challenges in processing visual information can lead to difficulties reading facial expressions and body language, key components of nonverbal social cues.

Overcoming Learning Disabilities

Improving social cue interpretation for individuals with learning disabilities involves targeted strategies tailored to each specific disability:

- **For Dyslexia:**
    - ***Enhanced Reading Practice:*** Engage in structured and systematic reading programs focusing on phonemic awareness and phonics.
    - ***Use of Assistive Technology:*** Tools like text-to-speech software can help interpret written social cues more accurately.
    - ***Visual Aids:*** Incorporate visual aids that can help understand and organize written information, aiding in interpreting written social cues.

- **For Dysgraphia:**
    - ***Occupational Therapy:*** Occupational therapy can help improve fine motor skills, making writing clearer and more effective for communication.
    - ***Use Dictation Software:*** Dictation software can aid in communicating more effectively in writing.
    - ***Alternative Communication Methods:*** Encourage using other forms of communication, such as verbal or visual aids, where appropriate.

- **For Dyscalculia:**
  - ***Mathematical Reasoning Therapy:*** Specialized math education programs can help understand sequences and patterns.
  - ***Use Concrete Examples:*** Applying mathematical concepts to real-life situations can improve understanding.
  - ***Visual and Practical Learning Aids:*** Utilize visual aids and practical examples to make abstract concepts more tangible.

- **For Auditory Processing Disorder (APD):**
  - ***Auditory Training:*** Programs that focus on improving listening skills can be beneficial.
  - ***Environmental Adjustments:*** Reduce background noise and use sound-amplifying devices to improve auditory input.
  - ***Visual Supports:*** Rely on visual cues and written communication to supplement auditory information.

- **For Visual Processing Disorder (VPD):**
  - ***Visual Therapy:*** Engage in activities designed to improve visual processing skills.
  - ***Use of High-Contrast Materials:*** Employ materials with high visual contrast to enhance visual perception.
  - ***Structured Learning Environments:*** Organize learning and social environments to minimize visual confusion.

Additionally, for all these disabilities:

- **Social Skills Training:** Specific training in social skills can help individuals recognize and respond to social cues more effectively.
- **Counseling and Therapy:** Counseling can help develop coping strategies and improve social interaction skills.
- **Peer Support Groups:** Engaging with others who have similar challenges can provide practical tips and emotional support.

These strategies aim to enhance the individual's ability to process and respond to social cues, improving communication and interaction in social settings.

Chapter 3

Authenticity

In a world where superficial interactions have become the norm, authenticity stands out as a beacon of genuine connection. Authenticity in communication is about being true to yourself and sincerely expressing thoughts, emotions, and values. When you communicate authentically, you create a space that encourages trust, understanding, and engagement.

Benefits of Authenticity

Being authentic brings a lot of benefits with it, such as:

Deeper Connection

One of authenticity's benefits is allowing others to connect with you more deeply. When you communicate authentically, you show vulnerability and open yourself to genuine human connections. People appreciate authenticity because it shows that you are being real and transparent. Doing so creates an environment where others feel safe to be themselves and share their thoughts and feelings.

Building Trust

Authentic communication also helps in building trust. When you are authentic, you are seen as reliable and trustworthy. Being honest and genuine in your interactions builds trust, strengthening relationships. Trust is essential for engaging communication because it allows for open and honest dialogue, enabling deeper understanding and collaboration.

Deeper Connection

Another thing it does is that it encourages empathy and understanding. When you communicate authentically, you can better connect with others on an emotional level. By sharing your experiences, challenges, and triumphs, you create common ground and enable others to relate to you. This shared understanding promotes empathy as you recognize and validate others' emotions, perspectives, and experiences.

Accepting Your Uniqueness

Being authentic also means embracing imperfections and being comfortable with your uniqueness. It frees you from the pressure of trying to fit a mold or conform to societal expectations. When you accept yourself as you are, you allow others to do the same. This acceptance creates an atmosphere of acceptance and inclusivity, which cultivates engagement and collaboration.

Components of Authenticity

Authenticity has different components, and learning about it helps you apply this skill to your communications to make true and honest connections with others. These components are:

Self-Awareness

Self-awareness involves clearly understanding your values, beliefs, thoughts, feelings, strengths, and weaknesses without a shadow of a doubt about who you are, what you believe in, and what matters to you. When you are self-aware, you can be true to yourself rather than pretend to be someone else. Self-awareness allows you to communicate authentically, showing others the real you and building connections based on honesty and integrity.

Honesty and Transparency

Authentic communication thrives on honesty and transparency. It means speaking truthfully and openly sharing your thoughts, feelings, and experiences. Avoid the temptation to exaggerate, manipulate, or hide information. Instead, be straightforward and genuine in your interactions.

Vulnerability

Authenticity also requires embracing your vulnerability. It means allowing yourself to be seen, heard, and understood in your raw and genuine state. Being vulnerable is scary as it is challenging because being open means sharing your fears, insecurities, and imperfections with others. But when you show your vulnerability, you invite others to do the same, creating a space for authentic and engaging communication.

Consistency

Consistency, concerning authenticity, means staying true to yourself and your values in all aspects of your life. It involves aligning your words, actions, and values at all times. Inconsistent behavior or contradictory messages can create confusion and erode trust. When you are consistent, people can trust that you will be the same person in different situations. It shows that you are genuine and reliable. Strive to communicate consistently and authentically, ensuring harmonious words and actions.

Respect and Acceptance

Being authentic also entails respecting others' differences and accepting them for this. It means honoring their opinions, values, and experiences, even if they differ from your own. Treat others with kindness, empathy, and an open mind. Avoid judgment, criticism, or dismissive attitudes. By respecting and accepting others, you create an inclusive and supportive environment that encourages engaging communication.

Cultivating Authenticity

Below are additional practical strategies to help you become a more authentic conversationalist and unlock the power of genuine communication.

Practice Self-Reflection

Take the time to reflect on your values, beliefs, and strengths. Understand what truly matters to you and how you want to show up. Through self-reflection, you become more aware of who you are. This, in turn, helps you align your actions with your authentic self.

Be Mindful of Social Expectations

Society often imposes expectations on how one should behave and communicate. Be aware of these expectations to prevent them from overshadowing your authenticity. Stay true to yourself, even if it means going against societal norms. Authenticity is about being genuine and unique, not conforming to others' expectations.

Embrace Imperfections

Authenticity means embracing your imperfections and being comfortable with your flaws. Nobody is perfect, and making mistakes or having shortcomings is normal. Embrace them as part of your unique journey and learn from them. By embracing your imperfections, you also create a space for others to embrace their imperfections.

Surround Yourself with Authenticity

Cultivate authenticity by surrounding yourself with people who appreciate and encourage genuine communication. Build relationships with individuals who value authenticity and create an environment supporting you for being true to yourself.

Embrace authenticity by practicing these strategies. Use it as a guiding principle in your communication, and watch as your relationships flourish and your connections deepen.

Book 3
The Art of Storytelling

Using Compelling Narratives for Persuasion, Inspiration, and Connection

Table of Contents

Chapter 1

Understanding Compelling Narratives

A compelling narrative concerning effective communication is a story or message that captures the attention and engages the emotions of the audience. It is crafted to captivate and resonate with your listeners, drawing them into the narrative and leaving a lasting impact.

Benefits

If done properly, a compelling narrative can strengthen the effectiveness of your communication. Here are the benefits that you will reap by improving your storytelling.

Enhancing Engagement

Unlike dry facts and statistics, stories create an emotional connection that keeps the audience actively involved. Presenting your information in a compelling narrative format can capture attention, maintain interest, and make your message more memorable. Engaged listeners are more likely to be receptive to your ideas and open to persuasion.

Simplifying Complex Concepts

Complex concepts refer to abstract or intricate ideas, theories, or topics that people may struggle to grasp or understand initially. These concepts can be challenging to convey in a straightforward manner, especially when they involve technical, philosophical, or nuanced subject matter. However, storytelling uniquely simplifies and makes these complex concepts more accessible and relatable to the audience.

Through the power of narrative, stories can provide tangible examples, emotional connections, and engaging experiences that help individuals comprehend and internalize complex ideas more effectively. With narratives, you can break down intricate concepts into relatable and understandable stories using metaphors, analogies, and vivid descriptions. By weaving complex concepts into compelling stories, you can bridge the gap between knowledge and understanding, making it easier for your audience to grasp and apply these concepts in their lives.

Fostering Memorable Communication

Humans are wired to remember stories. Storytelling's narrative structure helps people remember and recall information more effectively. By weaving facts and information into a compelling story, you create a mental anchor for your audience. This enhances their ability to retain and recall the key points long after the communication has ended.

When delivering a presentation, pitching a business idea, or seeking to influence others, incorporating compelling stories into your communication strategy can elevate your message, captivate your audience, and drive desired outcomes.

Types

In effective communication, narratives can engage, inspire, and connect with an audience. A well-crafted story can evoke emotions, convey messages, and leave a lasting impact. There are various types of compelling narratives, such as:

Personal Stories

A personal story refers to a narrative based on the experiences, emotions, and perspectives of the storyteller. Personal stories draw from the storyteller's life, highlighting significant events, challenges, triumphs, or lessons they have encountered. These stories often evoke a sense of authenticity and relatability as they glimpse the storyteller's personal growth, values, and beliefs. These stories have a powerful impact on the audience, creating an emotional connection and allowing individuals to see themselves reflected in the narrative. Storytellers can engage their audience deeper by sharing personal stories, fostering empathy, understanding, and a sense of shared humanity.

How to Use Personal Stories Effectively

The impact of personal stories cannot be underestimated, as they possess a unique ability to captivate and engage listeners, making them an invaluable tool in effective communication. Understand how to utilize personal stories to their fullest potential with these tips:

- **Choose the right story for your audience.** Selecting a personal story that resonates with your listeners is essential to connect deeply with them. Consider their background, experiences, and interests when sharing a story. By aligning your narrative with their emotions and values, you can create a stronger bond and make your message more meaningful.

- **Craft your story based on the message.** Every personal story should have a purpose and a clear message that you want to convey. Reflect on what you aim to communicate and select a story that best aligns with that objective. This way, your story becomes a powerful vehicle for conveying your intended message, making it more impactful and memorable.

- **Adapt the story to the setting.** Different storytelling settings call for different approaches. When speaking in a formal conference, an intimate gathering, or even a casual conversation, consider how to adapt your personal story accordingly. Adjust the tone, language, and level of detail to suit the specific setting and ensure that your story resonates with your listeners in that particular context.

- **Keep it concise and focused.** In the fast-paced world where attention spans are limited, brevity is key. Aim to keep your personal stories short and focused, lasting only a few minutes. Trim unnecessary details or tangents to maintain the audience's engagement and ensure your story effectively delivers its core message.

- **Practice for natural delivery.** Practice makes perfect, and this applies to storytelling too. The more you rehearse telling your personal story, the more comfortable and natural it will sound. Practice in front of a mirror or with a friend, refining your delivery and finding the right rhythm. This way, sharing your story will flow effortlessly, enhancing its impact.

Case Studies

Case studies involve an in-depth examination of a specific situation, problem, or scenario. It involves presenting real-life examples or instances to illustrate a particular concept, principle, or outcome. Case studies are often used to provide evidence, support arguments, or demonstrate the effectiveness of a particular approach or strategy. They typically present detailed information about the context, individuals involved, challenges faced, and the solutions or outcomes achieved. Case studies help to make abstract or complex concepts more tangible and relatable by showcasing how they play out in real-world situations. By sharing case studies, you can provide concrete evidence and practical insights, helping the audience better understand and apply the communicated ideas.

How to Use Case Studies Effectively

When presenting to a small group, delivering a speech, or writing an article, using case studies effectively can help you engage your audience, provide evidence-based examples, and reinforce your key points. This guide will provide you with practical strategies on how to use case studies effectively.

- **Choose Relevant and Compelling Case Studies**. Select case studies that are relevant to your topic or message. Look for compelling, relatable stories that align with your audience's interests and experiences. Ensure that the case studies are based on real-life situations and clearly demonstrate the points you want to make.

- **Set the Context.** When introducing a case study, provide the necessary background information to set the context. Explain the situation, problem, or challenge faced by the individuals or organizations involved. Help your audience understand the significance and relevance of the case study to the topic.

- **Tell a Compelling Story**. Craft your case study as a narrative that captures attention and maintains interest. Use vivid and descriptive language to paint a picture of the situation and the individuals involved. Engage your audience by presenting the story in a way that evokes emotions and stimulates their imagination.

- **Highlight Key Points and Lessons Learned**. Focus on the key points and lessons that can be derived from the case study. Clearly articulate the insights, strategies, or solutions implemented and their outcomes. Emphasize the relevance and applicability of these findings to your audience's lives, work, or interests.

- **Provide Supporting Evidence**. Support your case study with relevant data, facts, or statistics to bolster your arguments. Include testimonials, quotes, or feedback from individuals involved in the case study to add credibility and authenticity. Use visuals such as charts, graphs, or images to make the information more engaging and memorable.

- **Encourage Audience Participation**. Engage your audience by encouraging their active participation. Pose thought-provoking questions about the case study and invite them to share their perspectives, insights, or experiences. This creates a dynamic and interactive environment, fostering deeper engagement and understanding.

- **Relate the Case Study to Your Main Message**. Link the case study back to your main message or topic. Clearly explain how the lessons learned from the case study align with your overall objective. Emphasize the practical applications and implications of the case study's findings, highlighting how they support or reinforce your message.

- **Reflect and Summarize**. After presenting the case study, take a moment to reflect on the key learnings and insights. Summarize the main points and provide a concise takeaway that reinforces your message. Encourage your audience to reflect on how they can apply the lessons from the case study to their own lives or work.

Using case studies effectively can significantly enhance your communication skills and make your message more impactful. By practicing these strategies, you can captivate your audience, inspire action, and leave a lasting impression.

Metaphorical Narratives

A metaphorical narrative is a type of storytelling that uses metaphors or symbolic language to convey a deeper meaning or message. Instead of presenting information directly, a metaphorical narrative engages the audience by painting a vivid picture or creating an analogy that resonates with their experiences and emotions. It allows complex concepts or abstract ideas to be communicated in a relatable and accessible way, making it easier for the audience to grasp and remember. Metaphorical narratives often evoke powerful imagery and emotions, enabling a deeper connection with the audience and enhancing the impact of the communication.

How to Use Metaphorical Narratives Effectively

Here are some techniques on how to utilize metaphorical narrative effectively.

- **Understand your message**. Before incorporating a metaphorical narrative, clearly understand the message you want to convey. Identify the key points and concepts you want to emphasize and consider how they can be metaphorically represented.

- **Choose appropriately.** Select metaphors that align with your message and resonate with your audience. Consider using familiar objects, situations, or experiences that can easily be understood and related to by your listeners.

- **Paint a vivid picture.** Use descriptive language to paint a vivid picture in the minds of your audience. Engage their senses and create a mental image that captures the essence of your message. This will help make the metaphorical narrative more engaging and memorable.

- **Make it relatable**. Connect the metaphor to real-life situations or experiences your audience can relate to. By linking the metaphorical narrative to their personal lives, you increase the likelihood of them understanding and internalizing the message.

- **Create emotional impact**. Use metaphors that evoke emotions and tap into the emotional aspects of your audience. This can help create a deeper connection and engagement with your message. Consider the emotional tone you want to convey and select metaphors that align with that tone.

- **Use storytelling techniques.** Incorporate techniques such as characters, plot, and conflict into your metaphorical narrative. This will help make it more engaging and captivating for your audience.

- **Practice and refine.** Practice delivering your metaphorical narrative to ensure a smooth and impactful delivery. Pay attention to your tone, pacing, and body language to enhance the overall effectiveness of your communication.

- **Gauge audience response.** Pay attention to how your audience responds to your metaphorical narrative. Observe their reactions, engage in dialogue, and be open to feedback. This will help you gauge the effectiveness of your communication and make any necessary adjustments.

Using metaphorical narrative effectively engages your audience, conveys complex concepts, and leaves a lasting impression. Remember to be intentional with your metaphors and strive to create a meaningful and relatable experience for your listeners.

Historical Narratives

Historical narratives are a type of storytelling that involves recounting past events and experiences in a compelling and engaging manner. These narratives draw upon historical facts, figures, and events to convey a message or lesson. By weaving together historical context, characters, and plot, historical narratives provide a rich and immersive experience that helps the audience understand and appreciate the significance of the past. It allows your audience to learn from history, gain insights into human experiences, and draw parallels to contemporary issues. Historical narratives can be a powerful tool for effective communication, as they provide a sense of connection to the past and offer valuable lessons that resonate well with the present.

How to Use Historical Narratives Effectively

Using historical narratives effectively for effective communication requires careful planning and execution. Here are strategies that can guide you in harnessing the power of historical narratives in your communication:

- **Research and Select Relevant Historical Events**. Choose events that connect clearly to the points you want to make or the lessons you want to convey.

- **Craft a Compelling Storyline**. Develop a storyline that captures the essence of the historical event and engages your audience. Create compelling characters, build tension, and include key plot points that highlight the significance of the event. Use vivid descriptions and sensory details to bring the story to life.

- **Provide Context and Background Information.** Before delving into the narrative, provide sufficient context and background information about the historical event. Explain the historical setting, the key players involved, and the social, cultural, or political climate of the time. This helps the audience understand the significance and relevance of the story.

- **Draw Parallels to the Present.** Connect the historical narrative to present-day issues or challenges. Highlight the similarities or lessons that can be learned from the past and apply them to current situations. This helps your audience relate to the narrative and see its relevance in their own lives.

- **Use Visual Aids and Multimedia.** Incorporate visual aids, such as images, maps, or videos, to enhance the storytelling experience. These visuals can help the audience visualize the historical context, locations, or key events. Additionally, consider using multimedia elements like music or sound effects to create a more immersive and engaging experience.

- **Emphasize the Human Element.** Focus on the human stories within the historical narrative. Highlight the experiences, emotions, and motivations of the individuals involved. This personalizes the narrative and allows your audience to connect on an emotional level.

- **Highlight Key Takeaways or Lessons.** After sharing the historical narrative, emphasize the key takeaways or lessons that can be drawn from the story. Clearly articulate the message or insight you want your audience to gain from the historical event. This helps your audience to make connections between the past and the present.

- **Encourage Reflection and Discussion.** Create opportunities for reflection and discussion after sharing the historical narrative. Prompt your audience to think critically about the lessons learned and how they can be applied to their lives or current situations. Encourage open dialogue and invite questions to foster engagement and deeper understanding.

- **Practice and Refine.** Rehearse your delivery of the historical narrative to ensure clarity, pacing, and impact. Pay attention to your tone of voice, body language, and overall presentation. Seek feedback from trusted individuals to refine and improve your storytelling skills.

Inspirational Stories

Inspiring stories are a type of storytelling that aims to uplift, motivate, and ignite positive emotions within the audience. These stories often focus on individuals or groups who have overcome challenges, achieved remarkable success, or demonstrated extraordinary resilience. Inspiring stories captivate the audience's attention and evoke feelings of hope, determination, and empowerment. They serve as powerful tools for effective communication by providing examples of triumph over adversity and illustrating the potential for growth and transformation. Through inspiring stories, listeners are inspired to believe in their capabilities, embrace change, and pursue their goals with renewed vigor.

How to Use Inspiring Stories Effectively

Inspiring stories can drastically change how your audience hears and receives your message. Use these tips to use inspiring stories effectively:

- **Choose the right story**. Like other storytelling types, choosing the appropriate story is at the top of the list for effectively using these types. Always select a story that resonates with your message and your audience. For the inspiring type of stories, search for comparative stories that highlight perseverance, personal growth, or acts of kindness.

- **Craft a compelling narrative**. Structure your story to have a clear beginning, middle, and end. After introducing the main character, describe the challenges they faced and highlight their journey towards success or personal transformation.

- **Make it relatable.** Connect the story to your audience's experiences and emotions. Highlight the universal themes or values everyone can identify with, such as courage, resilience, or pursuing dreams.

- **Create emotional impact.** Use vivid and descriptive language to evoke emotions. Show the struggles, setbacks, and triumphs of the characters to create an emotional connection with your listeners.

- **Focus on the positive.** Emphasize the positive aspects of the story, such as the lessons learned, personal growth, or the impact on others. Inspiring stories should leave the audience feeling uplifted and motivated.

- **Be authentic.** Share stories that are genuine and truthful. Authenticity adds credibility to your message and helps the audience connect with your story on a deeper level.

- **Use visuals and multimedia.** Incorporate visuals, such as images or videos, to enhance the impact of your story. Multimedia elements can make the story more engaging and memorable.

- **Connect the story to your message.** After sharing the inspiring story, relate it to your main message or purpose. Explain how the story aligns with the ideas or values you want to convey.

- **Encourage reflection and action.** Prompt your audience to reflect on the story and how it applies to their lives. Encourage them to take action or make positive changes based on the inspiration they gained from the story.

- **Practice and refine.** Practice telling your story to ensure a smooth delivery. Pay attention to your tone, pacing, and gestures to create a captivating presentation.

Humorous Narratives

A humorous narrative is a form of storytelling that utilizes humor and wit to engage and entertain the audience. It involves sharing funny anecdotes, jokes, or comical situations to captivate the listeners' attention. Humor adds an element of enjoyment and lightness to the narrative, making it more memorable and relatable. It can help break down barriers, create a positive and engaging atmosphere, and establish a connection with the audience. Humorous narratives are especially effective in presentations, speeches, or any form of communication where you want to leave a lasting impression while fostering a sense of enjoyment and lightheartedness. However, strike the right balance and consider the appropriateness of humor for the specific context and audience.

How to Use Humorous Narrative Effectively

Employing humor in your story can make your message more memorable and create a positive and engaging atmosphere. Here are some strategies to effectively incorporate humorous narratives into your communication.

- **Know your audience**. Understand the preferences, cultural backgrounds, and sensitivities of your audience. Tailor your humor to resonate with them and avoid offensive or controversial jokes.

- **Be authentic.** Use humor that aligns with your personality and style. Authenticity makes the humor more genuine and relatable, building trust and connection with your audience.

- **Choose the right moments.** Identify appropriate opportunities to inject humor into your narrative. Use it to lighten the mood, introduce a topic, or provide a humorous anecdote that supports your message.

- **Keep it relevant.** Ensure that your humor directly relates to the topic or message you want to convey. This connection will help reinforce your point and make it more memorable.

- **Use storytelling techniques.** Craft a well-structured narrative with a clear setup, punchline, and resolution. Use vivid descriptions, engaging characters, and unexpected twists to make the humor more effective.

- **Practice delivery.** Work on your timing, tone, and delivery to enhance the comedic impact. Practice your humorous narratives to ensure they are delivered with confidence and precision.

- **Balance humor and seriousness**. Remember that your primary goal is effective communication. While humor can engage and entertain, it does not overshadow the main message. Find a balance between humor and the serious aspects of your communication.

- **Gauge audience response**. Pay attention to the reactions of your audience. If they enjoy and respond positively to the humor, you can continue with a similar tone. If not, adjust your approach accordingly.

- **Avoid offensive or divisive humor.** Be mindful of cultural, social, or personal sensitivities. Avoid offensive or divisive jokes or narratives that can undermine your communication goals.

- **Practice moderation**. Use humor sparingly and strategically. Too much humor can distract from your message, while too little can dull your communication. Find the right balance based on the context and desired outcome.

Visionary Narratives

A visionary narrative is a type of storytelling that paints a vivid and compelling picture of a desirable future or a bold vision. It involves sharing a story that inspires and motivates the audience to imagine a better world, embrace change, and take action. A visionary narrative taps into people's aspirations, dreams, and hopes, helping them see beyond the present challenges and envision a brighter future. It often includes inspiration, innovation, and possibility, captivating the audience's imagination and stirring their emotions. By sharing a visionary narrative, communicators can inspire others to join their cause, rally support for a vision, and drive positive societal change.

How to Use Visionary Narratives Effectively

Here are some techniques to help you master the power of visionary narratives. Refer to these strategies because while powerful, visionary narratives require careful consideration and strategic planning.

- **Define your vision**. Clearly articulate the future you envision and the positive impact it will have. Identify the core values and goals that underpin your vision.

- **Understand your audience**. Research and understand the hopes, dreams, and aspirations of your target audience. Tailor your narrative to resonate with their values and desires.

- **Craft a compelling story.** Develop a narrative that engages the audience emotionally and intellectually. Start with a captivating introduction that captures their attention and sets the stage for your vision.

- **Paint a vivid picture**. Use vivid and descriptive language to create a sensory experience for the audience. Help them visualize and emotionally connect with the future you are portraying.

- **Appeal to emotions.** Stir emotions by highlighting the positive impact and benefits of your vision. Use storytelling techniques such as personal anecdotes, powerful metaphors, and relatable characters to engage the audience's emotions.

- **Make it relatable.** Ground your visionary narrative in real-world examples and practical scenarios. Connect your vision to the everyday lives of your audience, showing them how they can be a part of the transformation.

- **Show the path forward.** Provide a clear and actionable roadmap for achieving the vision. Outline the steps, resources, and support needed to make the vision a reality.

- **Be authentic and inspiring.** Speak from the heart and convey your passion and belief in the vision. Share personal experiences and genuine stories that illustrate the transformative power of your vision.

- **Use visuals and multimedia.** Enhance your narrative with visuals, videos, or other multimedia elements that reinforce the key messages and bring your vision to life.

- **Engage in dialogue.** Encourage interaction and dialogue with your audience. Listen to their perspectives, address their concerns, and invite them to contribute ideas and insights.

- **Amplify your message**. Leverage various communication channels such as public speaking, social media, blogs, or videos to reach a wider audience and create a buzz around your vision.

- **Measure and adjust.** Continuously evaluate the impact of your visionary narrative. Seek feedback, monitor engagement, and make adjustments as necessary to ensure your communication remains effective.

By following this guide, you can tap into the power of visionary narratives to inspire, motivate, and mobilize your audience toward a shared vision of a better future.

Chapter 2

Overcoming Challenges

Storytelling is a powerful tool for communication, allowing us to engage and influence our audience. However, like any skill, it comes with its own set of challenges and potential pitfalls. In this chapter, discover the common obstacles faced in storytelling.

Resistance and Skepticism

Resistance and skepticism refer to the barriers or doubts that individuals may have when receiving and processing your story.

Resistance can arise when the audience has pre-existing beliefs, biases, or emotional reactions that hinder their acceptance of your story's message. ***Skepticism***, on the other hand, involves a general attitude of doubt or questioning towards the story's credibility or relevance.

Some of the most common kinds of resistance include:

Cognitive Dissonance

Cognitive dissonance occurs when individuals encounter information that contradicts their beliefs or values. To address this type of resistance, start by establishing common ground. Find areas of agreement or shared values and build upon them. Present your ideas in a manner that aligns with their worldview, making it easier for them to accept your message. Additionally, provide compelling evidence and logical reasoning to bridge the gap between their current beliefs and the ideas you are presenting.

Emotional Resistance

Emotional resistance arises when individuals have strong emotional reactions or biases that hinder their acceptance of your message. To overcome emotional resistance, focus on building empathy and connection. Share personal stories or anecdotes that evoke emotions and resonate with their experiences. Use language that appeals to their emotions, demonstrating that you understand and empathize with their concerns. Engage in active listening and validate their emotions, creating a safe space for them to open up and consider alternative perspectives.

Skepticism and Distrust

Skepticism and distrust often stem from a lack of confidence in the communicator or the presented information. To address this type of resistance, establish credibility and trustworthiness from the outset. Share your expertise and credentials and provide evidence of your knowledge and experience in the subject matter.

Use reliable and reputable sources to back up your claims. Incorporate testimonials or success stories from individuals who have benefited from your ideas or solutions. Building trust and credibility can alleviate skepticism and foster a receptive attitude.

Cultural or Ideological Differences

Cultural or ideological differences can create resistance when individuals perceive your message as incompatible with their cultural or ideological beliefs. To address this resistance, demonstrate cultural sensitivity and respect for diverse perspectives. Tailor your message to resonate with their cultural values or ideologies, highlighting how your ideas align with their core principles. Avoid judgment or criticism and instead focus on finding common ground and shared goals. Encourage open dialogue and constructive conversations that promote understanding and bridge cultural divides.

Lack of Relevance or Personal Connection

Resistance may also arise when individuals perceive your message as irrelevant to their lives or fail to establish a personal connection. To overcome this, emphasize the relevance and practicality of your ideas. Provide concrete examples or case studies illustrating how your message can positively impact their lives or address their needs. Tailor your communication to resonate with their experiences, using relatable language and relaying stories that they can connect with on a personal level.

Storytelling Mistakes

Certain mistakes can undermine a compelling narrative, including:

Lack of Clarity and Structure

- **Mistake**: A common storytelling mistake is a lack of clarity and structure, where the narrative lacks direction or a logical sequence, confusing the audience.

- **Strategy**: Outline the key points and main events of your story. Ensure a clear beginning, middle, and end, and use transitions to guide the flow. Focus on the main message and eliminate unnecessary details or digressions that can distract from the central theme.

Weak Character Development

- **Mistake:** Weak character development can diminish the impact of a story, making it challenging for the audience to connect and relate.

- **Strategy:** Invest time in developing your characters. Give them depth and complexity, making them relatable and engaging. Show their emotions, thoughts, and actions to make them come alive. Provide backstory and context to add depth to their journey and allow the audience to form a connection with them.

Lack of Conflict or Tension

- **Mistake:** A story without conflict or tension can be unengaging and fail to attract the audience.

- **Strategy:** Introduce and develop conflict early on to create suspense and intrigue. Establish obstacles and challenges the characters must overcome, building anticipation and driving the narrative forward. Increase tension through suspenseful moments, unexpected twists, or contrasting perspectives to keep the audience invested in the outcome.

Overloading with Information

- **Mistake:** Overloading the audience with excessive information can overwhelm and dilute the impact of the story.

- **Strategy:** Focus on key points and use concise language to convey necessary information. Prioritize relevance and eliminate unnecessary details. Use vivid descriptions, sensory language, and metaphors to engage the audience's imagination and convey information more engagingly and memorably.

Lack of Emotional Appeal

- **Mistake:** Stories that lack emotional appeal can fail to resonate with the audience.

- **Strategy:** Engage the audience's emotions by incorporating relatable experiences, personal anecdotes, and evocative language. Show vulnerability and authenticity, allowing the audience to connect with the story on an emotional level. Use descriptive language to evoke emotions and create a sensory experience. Appeal to emotions such as joy, sadness, empathy, or excitement to make the story more memorable and impactful.

Ethical Considerations or Sensitive Topics

Ethical considerations refer to the mindful and responsible approach taken by someone telling a story or narrative to uphold ethical principles and values. It involves considering the potential impact of the story on the audience and the broader society, ensuring fairness, accuracy, and respect for diverse perspectives. Ethical storytelling involves avoiding harmful stereotypes, promoting inclusivity, and being transparent about biases or limitations. As the communicator, it emphasizes your responsibility to prioritize the well-being and dignity of individuals and communities involved in or affected by your story. Show responsibility by handling the narrative with the utmost care and sensitivity.

Below are strategies on how to successfully navigate the sea of ethical considerations.

Research and Understanding

Research and understanding, in storytelling, means learning as much as possible about the topic at hand. It requires delving into various sources, gathering reliable information, and seeking multiple perspectives to develop a comprehensive understanding of the subject. By researching, you can ensure that you are factual, helping you avoid misrepresentation or harmful stereotypes and allowing you to discuss sensitive topics accurately.

Take the time to ensure you get information from credible sources. Likewise, understanding goes beyond surface-level knowledge. It involves engaging with communities or individuals directly affected by the subject matter. Develop empathy and gain insight into the nuances and complexities surrounding the topic before incorporating it into your storytelling.

Invest time and effort in research and understanding to approach your narrative creation with care and sensitivity, contributing to a more ethical and responsible storytelling process.

Respectful Portrayal

Respectful portrayal means treating the people and cultures in the story with fairness and dignity. It involves representing them in a way that is accurate and respectful. It means avoiding harmful stereotypes. It conveys your understanding and value of their perspectives, experiences, and beliefs.

Respectful portrayal also means seeking permission when sharing their personal stories. Be mindful of the potential impact the story may have on them or their communities.

A strategy you can use is to create well-rounded and authentic characters that reflect the diversity and complexity of real-life experiences. If you can, avoid generalizations or oversimplifications and seek input or feedback from individuals or communities connected to the topic to ensure respectful and accurate portrayal.

Balancing Emotional Impact

Sensitive topics often evoke strong emotions. Balancing emotional impact means being mindful of the emotions a story evokes in the audience. It involves carefully considering the potential effects of the story on individuals' feelings and well-being. While storytelling often aims to engage and move the audience emotionally, it is important to strike a balance and not exploit or manipulate emotions for personal gain.

As an ethical storyteller and communicator, you must create an emotional connection while ensuring the impact is respectful, responsible, and empathetic. Consider the potential vulnerability of the audience and approach emotional themes with sensitivity and care. Balancing emotional impact can create a meaningful and thought-provoking experience without causing harm or distress.

Use storytelling techniques like framing, context, and thoughtful language to responsibly guide the audience's emotional journey.

Transparency

Transparency means being honest, genuine, and upfront with your audience. It is especially important, particularly when discussing sensitive topics. It involves sharing information openly and acknowledging any biases or conflicts of interest that may affect the story. Transparency ensures that the audience understands the context and can make informed judgments.

Be transparent about your intentions and motivations for addressing the sensitive topic. Acknowledge your own biases or limitations and strive for authenticity in portraying the experiences of others. Engage in open, honest dialogue with your audience to build trust and encourage constructive conversations.

Impact Assessment

Before sharing a story with sensitive content, consider its potential impact on the audience and broader community.

Impact assessment involves evaluating and understanding the potential effects of the story on individuals, communities, and society as a whole. It means considering the intended and unintended consequences of the narrative, both positive and negative. Impact assessment helps you as a storyteller identify and mitigate potential harm, such as reinforcing stereotypes, causing emotional distress, or perpetuating biases. It also helps you identify positive change opportunities, such as promoting empathy, raising awareness, or inspiring action. Do this assessment before sharing a story with sensitive content.

Follow these steps on how to conduct your impact assessments:

1. **Clearly define the purpose of the impact assessment.** Identify the specific goals, objectives, and intended out-

comes of the storytelling initiative. Determine the scope of the assessment, including the target audience, geographic reach, and timeframe.

2. **Identify the different areas that may be impacted by the storytelling**, such as individuals' emotions, perceptions, attitudes, behaviors, or social norms. Consider the potential positive and negative impacts on individuals, communities, and society.

3. **Collect relevant data and information to assess the potential impact.** May include conducting surveys, interviews, focus groups, or literature reviews. Seek input from diverse perspectives and stakeholders to gain a comprehensive understanding of the potential effects.

4. **Analyze the collected data and information to identify patterns, trends, and themes.** Assess the potential risks, benefits, and unintended consequences of the storytelling initiative. Consider how the narrative may intersect with different cultural, social, and political contexts.

5. **Evaluate the impact assessment findings** to determine the significance and likelihood of the identified impacts. Consider the alignment of the impacts with the ethical considerations and desired outcomes. Assess the feasibil-

ity of mitigating any potential negative impacts and enhancing the positive ones.

6. Based on the evaluation of the impact assessment findings, **develop strategies to mitigate any potential negative impacts and enhance the positive ones.** This may involve adjusting the storytelling approach, addressing biases or stereotypes, providing additional support or resources, or collaborating with relevant stakeholders.

7. **Implement the identified strategies and closely monitor the impact of the storytelling initiative.** Continuously assess and reassess the impact throughout the implementation process. Gather feedback from the audience and stakeholders to inform ongoing improvements and adjustments.

8. **Reflect on the impact assessment process and outcomes.** Identify lessons learned and best practices for future storytelling initiatives. Share the findings and insights with relevant stakeholders to contribute to the broader field of ethical storytelling and effective communication.

Chapter 3

Crafting Compelling Narratives

Writing a compelling narrative significantly impacts effective communication by captivating the audience's attention and engaging their emotions. A well-crafted narrative helps you convey complex ideas, making them more relatable and memorable. Using vivid language, relatable examples, and storytelling techniques, a compelling narrative draws the audience in, enhances their understanding, and inspires them to take action. It creates a powerful connection, making communication more impactful and facilitating you to achieve the desired outcomes.

A compelling narrative has a *clear structure, relatable characters,* and a *meaningful message,* all working together to create a memorable and persuasive experience. It helps connect you, the communicator, and the audience.

Elements

Below are the elements of writing compelling narratives.

Storytelling Structure

A compelling narrative follows a structure that captures the attention of the audience and keeps them engaged. It typically includes an introduction to set the stage, a well-developed plot that builds anticipation, a climax that creates tension and emotional resonance, and a resolution that satisfies the audience's curiosity or leaves them with a powerful message.

Characters and Conflict

Characters bring the narrative to life and make it relatable to the audience. They have goals and motivations and face challenges or conflicts that drive the story forward. Compelling characters are well-developed and relatable and evoke empathy or emotional connection from the audience.

Clear Message or Theme

A compelling narrative often has a clear message or theme that is communicated effectively. It provides the audience a takeaway or a call to action, inspiring them to think, feel, or act differently. The message should be relatable, relevant, and meaningful to the audience, resonating with their values, beliefs, or experiences.

Visual Imagery

Visual imagery helps the audience visualize the story, making it more immersive and memorable. Well-crafted descriptions and sensory details can paint a picture in the minds of the listeners, heightening their engagement and connection to the narrative.

Descriptive language uses sensory details to create a vivid picture in the reader's mind. Create tangible imagery through this. For example, you could say, *"The air was thick with the smell of smoke,"* to create a sensory image of a smoky room.

Some tips for using descriptive language effectively in your storytelling are the following:

- **Be specific and concrete.**
    - *"The old man was bent over."* **(vague)**
    - *"The old man's back was hunched over like a question mark."* **(specific)**
    - *"The city was beautiful."* **(vague)**
    - *"The city's skyline was a breathtaking sight, with tall skyscrapers reaching up into the sky like a forest of steel."* **(specific)**

- **Incorporate sensory details for a vivid image.**
    - *"The rain fell in sheets."* **(general)**
    - *"The raindrops pelted my skin like hail, and the sound of the downpour was deafening."* **(specific)**

- **Embrace creativity and explore diverse descriptive techniques.**
    - *"The sun was setting."* **(simple)**
    - *"The sun sank below the horizon, casting a fiery glow across the sky."* **(more creative)**

Authenticity and Relatability

A compelling narrative is authentic and relatable to the audience. It reflects the communicator's genuine experiences, values, or perspectives, which helps build trust and credibility. By sharing relatable stories and emotions, the audience can connect with you on a deeper level, fostering a sense of understanding and resonance.

Engaging Delivery

How the narrative is delivered also plays a vital role in its effectiveness. By using intentional vocal techniques, you can enhance your storytelling. A skilled communicator uses tone, pacing, and body language to boost the impact of the story. Engaging delivery captivates the audience, holding their attention and creating a memorable experience.

There are several intentional vocal techniques that you can use to make your narratives more compelling. These techniques can be used to create a sense of excitement, suspense, humor, or any other emotion.

Utilize Tone, Pitch, and Melody

The voice can create a wide range of emotions and effects. Tell more engaging and memorable stories by varying your tone, pitch, and melody.

Tone refers to the overall mood or feeling of your voice and can create excitement, sadness, anger, or any other emotion. ***Pitch*** refers to the highness or lowness of your voice that creates a sense of suspense, mystery, or humor. ***Melody***, on the other hand, refers to the rhythm and pattern of your voice. It can create a sense of beauty, excitement, or calmness.

Here are a few tips for using tone, pitch, and melody in storytelling:

- **Vary your tone to create interest and excitement.** For example, you could use a louder, more excited tone when telling a suspenseful story.

- **Use a lower pitch to create a sense of mystery or suspense.** For example, you could use a lower pitch when telling a ghost story.

- **Use a higher pitch to create a sense of humor or lightness.** For example, you could use a higher pitch when telling a joke.

- **Use melody to create a sense of beauty, excitement, or calmness.** For example, you could use a flowing melody when telling a love story.

Use Pacing and Pauses

Pacing and pauses can also add emphasis and impact to your storytelling. By slowing down or pausing at key moments, you can draw attention to important details and create a sense of suspense or mystery in your narrative.

Here are a few tips for using pacing and pauses in storytelling:

- **Slow down or pause at key moments to add emphasis.** For example, you could slow down or pause when telling a character's name or revealing a plot twist.

- **Speed up your pacing** to create a sense of suspense, or slow down your pacing to create a sense of mystery.

- **Use pauses to allow your audience to absorb what you have just said.** Doing so can help them to understand the story and connect with the characters.

Incorporate Gestures and Movement

Gestures and movement can be used to enhance storytelling in several ways, such as:

- **Add emphasis and emotion to your words.** For example, you might use a sweeping gesture to indicate the size of a castle or a pounding fist to emphasize a character's anger.

- **Create a sense of atmosphere or mood.** For example, you might stand still and speak in a hushed voice to create a sense of suspense or pace back and forth to create a sense of excitement.

- **Help the audience visualize the story.** By using gestures and movement to describe the setting, characters, and action, you can help the audience create a mental picture of the story in their minds.

When incorporating gestures and movement into your storytelling, be aware of the following:

- **Be natural. Don't force your gestures or movements.** Let them flow naturally from your story.

- **Be mindful of your audience.** Ensure your gestures and movements are appropriate for the audience and setting.

- **Be expressive.** Use your gestures and movements to convey the emotions of your story.

Use Facial Expressions

Facial expressions convey emotions and reactions. Using your facial expressions to help the audience understand the characters' emotions is important when telling a story.

Some common facial expressions that can be used to convey emotions include:

- **Joy:** A smile, laugh, or twinkle in the eye
- **Sadness:** A frown, tears, or downcast eyes
- **Anger:** A scowl, clenched fists, or furrowed brow
- **Fear:** Wide eyes, a pale face, or rapid breathing
- **Surprise:** An open mouth, raised eyebrows, or a gasp

When using facial expressions to convey emotions, be aware of the following:

- **Be genuine.** Your facial expressions should be genuine and reflect the emotions of the characters.
- **Be subtle**. Do not overact with your facial expressions. A little can go a long way.
- **Be aware of your audience.** Make sure your facial expressions are appropriate for the audience and the setting.

Create a Dynamic Presence

In addition to gestures, movement, and facial expressions, your overall physicality can also contribute to your storytelling. Your posture, stance, and overall body language can all send messages to your audience. For example, if you want to appear confident and authoritative, you might stand up straight and make eye contact with your audience. When you want to appear relaxed and approachable, lean in and speak in a conversational tone.

When creating a dynamic presence through physicality, be aware of the following:

- **Be aware of your body language.** Your body language can send messages to your audience, so use it to your advantage.

- **Be comfortable in your skin.** The more comfortable you are with yourself, the more confident you will appear to your audience.

- **Be yourself.** Do not try to be someone you are not. Your audience will be able to tell, making you appear less genuine.

Process

Do the following to ensure you write a compelling narrative:

1. **Clarify the purpose of your narrative.** *What do you want to achieve with your communication?* **Define the key message you want to convey to your audience. Whether it is to inspire, educate, persuade, or entertain, a clear purpose will guide the direction of your narrative.**

2. **Understand who you are communicating with.** Consider their interests, values, and needs. Tailor your narrative to resonate with your specific audience. This will ensure that your story connects with them on a personal level and captures their attention.

3. **Craft a well-structured narrative to engage your audience.** Begin with a captivating introduction that hooks their interest. Establish the main conflict or challenge early on to create suspense. Develop the narrative through a sequence of events, building tension and excitement. Conclude with a powerful resolution or key takeaway that reinforces your message.

4. **Introduce relatable characters and provide context to make your narrative more vivid and engaging.** Develop characters with unique personalities and motivations. Set the stage by describing the setting, time, and place. Paint a visual picture for your audience, enabling them to immerse themselves in the story.

5. **Tap into the emotional aspect of storytelling.** Infuse your narrative with emotions that resonate with your audience. Emotions, such as joy, sadness, empathy, or excitement, will make your story more impactful and memorable. Use descriptive language and sensory details to evoke specific emotions.

6. **Introduce challenges, setbacks, or conflicts that create tension and suspense.** Every compelling narrative needs a conflict or obstacle to overcome. Show how your characters face these challenges and provide a resolution that aligns with your message. Highlight the lessons learned or growth experienced along the way.

7. **Make your narrative come alive with descriptive language and vivid imagery.** Paint a clear picture in the minds of your audience. Use metaphors, similes, and sensory details to create a sensory experience that immerses them in your story. The more vivid the imagery, the more engaging your narrative will be.

8. **Practice delivering your narrative through writing or speaking.** Pay attention to pacing, tone, and emphasis. Seek feedback from others and make adjustments to improve the impact and clarity of your story. Refining your storytelling skills takes practice, so be open to continuous learning and growth.

Structure

In writing compelling narratives, structure refers to the organization and arrangement of the story elements. It provides a framework that guides the flow and progression of the narrative. A well-crafted structure ensures the story has a clear beginning, middle, and end, with a logical sequence of events that builds tension and suspense. It helps to engage the audience by creating a sense of anticipation and coherence. A solid structure allows the narrative to unfold in a cohesive and compelling manner, keeping the audience captivated from start to finish.

Introduction

A captivating introduction is crucial for grabbing the audience's attention immediately. Do that by using a ***hook***, the opening element of a story that grabs the reader's or listener's attention. It is designed to captivate the audience from the beginning and compel them to continue reading or listening.

A hook can take various forms, such as a captivating statement, an intriguing question, a startling fact, or a vivid description. Its purpose is to create an immediate connection with the audience, pique their curiosity, and draw them into the narrative, setting the stage for an engaging storytelling experience.

Hooks can look like these:

> *"Are you tired of feeling overwhelmed by clutter? Discover the secret to an organized and stress-free life."*

> *"Looking for the perfect solution to boost your productivity and get more done in less time? Look no further."*

> *"Imagine a world where time travel is possible; you can journey back and witness history unfold before your eyes."*

> *"What if I told you everything you know about the world is a lie? That beneath the surface lies a hidden, extraordinary truth that will challenge everything you believe."*

"Have you ever wondered what it would be like to soar through the skies like a bird, to feel the wind rush against your face as you dive and twist through the clouds?"

"Discover the skincare revolution that will transform your complexion and leave you feeling radiant and confident."

Establish the Main Conflict

Establishing the primary challenge early on sets the stage for the narrative. It is a fundamental aspect of your storyline. This involves introducing a central problem, challenge, or tension the protagonist must confront and overcome. The conflict serves as the driving force that propels the story forward, creating intrigue and engaging the audience.

To effectively establish the main conflict, it is imperative to clearly define the stakes and make them relevant to the protagonist's desires, goals, or values. This can be done through various means, such as presenting opposing forces, introducing an obstacle or antagonist, or revealing an internal struggle within the protagonist.

By establishing the main conflict early on, the narrative gains momentum as your audience becomes emotionally invested in the resolution and eagerly anticipates how the protagonist will navigate the challenges they face.

Developing the Narrative

Develop the narrative through a sequence of events to add tension and build excitement to your story. When crafting a narrative for communication purposes, the goal is to engage the audience and deliver a compelling message. By structuring the story with a clear beginning, middle, and end, you, as the communicator, ensure that the narrative flows logically and keeps the audience's attention.

Each event in the sequence serves a purpose in advancing the story and reinforcing the message. It is important to carefully select and arrange the events to maintain a coherent and engaging narrative arc. The sequence of events helps to build anticipation, suspense, and emotional connection with the audience, making the communication more impactful and memorable. By developing the narrative through a well-crafted sequence of events, you can maintain the audience's interest and create a cohesive and satisfying storytelling experience for them, which can help you effectively convey your message.

Conclusion

Concluding with a powerful resolution or key takeaway serves as your final opportunity to leave a lasting impression on the audience and reinforce the main message or theme of your narrative. It should provide a sense of closure and satisfaction while leaving the audience with a clear takeaway or call to action.

A well-crafted conclusion ties up any loose ends and offers a resolution to the main conflict or challenge presented in your story. It can also provide a powerful and memorable ending, such as a thought-provoking statement, an inspiring quote, or a surprising twist. By carefully considering the conclusion, you ensure that the narrative is impactful and leaves a lasting impression, prompting the audience to reflect, take action, or continue the conversation.

For instance, imagine attending a business conference, and one of the speakers takes the stage. With a confident smile, she introduces herself, sharing a relatable story about her journey from a struggling entrepreneur to a successful business owner. This storytelling structure immediately captures your attention and piques your interest.

As the speaker continues, she introduces the main conflict she faced: the fear of failure and self-doubt. She shares her emotional journey of overcoming obstacles, pushing through challenges, and learning valuable lessons. You feel a sense of empathy and connection as she reveals vulnerable moments and shares how she overcame them.

Throughout her presentation, the speaker incorporates visual imagery by using descriptive language to paint vivid pictures. She describes the ups and downs, the highs and lows of her entrepreneurial journey, making it easy for you to visualize the obstacles she encountered and the triumphs she celebrated.

The speaker's authenticity shines through her genuine passion for her topic and her ability to share personal experiences. You can sense her sincerity, which builds trust and credibility. Her relatability creates a strong bond between her and the audience, making you feel inspired and motivated to take action.

As the presentation reaches its climax, the speaker delivers a clear message: failure is not the end but an opportunity for growth and success. She shares practical strategies and actionable advice, providing a roadmap to navigate challenges and achieve your goals.

The speaker's engaging style keeps you fully immersed in the narrative throughout her delivery. Her enthusiastic tone, animated gestures, and well-timed pauses add to the impact of her message. She knows how to hold your attention, making you feel energized and enthusiastic about the possibilities ahead.

This example demonstrates how communication can be elevated with a compelling narrative. By integrating the various elements of storytelling with the process and structure, a skilled communicator can deliver a powerful and memorable message, leaving a lasting impact on the audience.

Conclusion

As you come to the end of this transformative journey through the intricacies of effective communication, I am filled with a sense of gratitude and hope. Gratitude for the opportunity to share my knowledge and experiences with you, and hope that these insights will empower you to forge deeper connections, navigate social dynamics with confidence, and unlock the true potential of your relationships. My aim has been to offer a comprehensive guide in developing their practical skills, overcoming communication barriers, and using storytelling effectively.

Throughout this book, three major components of effective communication were discussed: *influence, interest,* and *storytelling.* In the first component, you have delved into the art of persuasion, understanding the power of influence, and using it ethically to create positive change. Later, you have uncovered the secrets of being interesting by mastering your social skills and getting familiar and intimate with social cues. Lastly, you discover the profound impact of storytelling by learning how to craft compelling narratives that captivate, inspire, and connect.

But this journey does not end with the final page of this book. Effective communication is a lifelong pursuit that requires practice, reflection, and continuous growth. The knowledge and strategies shared here will serve as a foundation, a springboard from which you can launch into a lifetime of meaningful communication.

Remember that effective communication is not just about the words you speak or the messages you convey. It is about the intention behind your words, the authenticity in your interactions, and the genuine connections you create. Understand and value the unique perspectives and experiences of others, as well as treat every interaction as an opportunity for growth and understanding.

As you master effective communication, embrace curiosity, remain open to learning, and practice self-reflection. Take the time to cultivate self-awareness to understand your strengths and areas for growth. Seek opportunities outside your comfort zone, engaging with diverse individuals and perspectives. Above all, be patient and kind to yourself as you navigate the challenges and celebrate successes.

Techniques and Tips Recap

The following techniques and tips are found in "Effective Communication [3 in 1]":

#	Name	Explanation
1	**Reciprocity**	Utilizing gifts to trigger a sense of reciprocity
2	**Strong Argumentation**	Use strong arguments, evidence, and narratives to enhance message persuasiveness.
3	**Effective Medium Selection**	Choose a communication medium that maximizes audience engagement.
4	**Audience-Aligned Messaging**	Tailor messages to resonate with the audience's values and concerns.
5	**Theory of Planned Behavior Utilization**	Create persuasive messages using the Theory of Planned Behavior to change behaviors.
6	**Social Identity Theory Application**	Tailor messages to appeal to the social identities of your audience.
7	**Addressing Social Identity Resistance**	Anticipate and address resistance from those with competing group identities.
8	**Authentic Communication**	Build trust and connections through authenticity and sincerity.

#	Name	Explanation
9	**Win-Win Solution Finding**	Create outcomes satisfying all parties involved for sustainable results.
10	**Knowledge Leverage**	Use your knowledge to establish trust and reliability.
11	**Balanced Assertiveness**	Maintain a balance between assertiveness and respecting others' views.
12	**Communication Style Adaptability**	Refine and expand your communication approach for different scenarios.
13	**Establishing Trust and Credibility**	Build trust and credibility through expertise, evidence, and reliability.
14	**Positive Emotional Elicitation**	Use communication to evoke positive emotions like joy and empathy.
15	**Highlighting Success Stories**	Use success stories to build confidence in your message.
16	**Anticipating Objections**	Prepare for potential objections and resistance in advance.
17	**Data-Driven Argument Strengthening**	Strengthen your case with data and real-life anecdotes.
18	**Respectful Dialogue Engagement**	Foster constructive atmosphere through respectful dialogue and well-reasoned arguments.
19	**Active Engagement**	Engage with people as much as possible for effective communication.

#	Name	Explanation
20	**Self-Esteem Building**	Boost self-esteem with realistic goals and a supportive network.
21	**Fear of Judgment Reduction**	Reduce fear of judgment through self-acceptance and social exposure.
22	**Challenging Limiting Beliefs**	Replace limiting beliefs with empowering ones by seeking counter-evidence and social support.
23	**Perspective Understanding**	Understand others' perspectives to reduce misinterpretations.
24	**Overcoming Communication Obstacles**	Identify and overcome environmental barriers to communication.
25	**Language Practice**	Practice speaking in various contexts and embrace mistakes as part of learning.
26	**Cultural Sensitivity Development**	Develop cultural sensitivity to enhance cross-cultural communication.
27	**Clarifying Questioning**	Ask questions for open and honest communication.
28	**Social Cue Decoding**	Improve social cue decoding by listening to variations in speech.
29	**Emotional Behavior Reflection**	Reflect on emotions to understand others' emotions better.
30	**Audience-Adaptive Communication**	Adapt communication style to meet audience needs.

#	Name	Explanation
31	**Contextual Reading**	Read between the lines by paying attention to context, word choice, and non-verbal cues.
32	**Emotional Vocabulary Enrichment**	Learn about various emotions and expressions to enhance social cue decoding.
33	**Self-Acceptance**	Accept yourself as you are to encourage others to do the same.
34	**Authentic Self-Expression**	Stay true to yourself, even against societal norms.
35	**Narrative Crafting**	Use compelling narrative formats to capture attention and make your message memorable.
36	**Focused Storytelling**	Keep personal stories short and focused for greater impact.
37	**Responsible Narrative Handling**	Handle narratives with care and sensitivity.
38	**Emotional Impact Balancing**	Balance emotional impact in storytelling for a meaningful experience.
39	**Narrative Tension Building**	Develop narratives through event sequences to build excitement.

Exclusive Bonuses

Dear Reader,

I am delighted to introduce to you an exclusive suite of bonuses that have been specially designed to complement and enhance your journey into mastering the art of communication. Each bonus is a unique tool, crafted to assist you in developing and refining your communication skills across various dimensions.

- **Bonus 1 - Strategic Persuasion: Persuasion Strategy Brainstorming Sheet**

  This brainstorming sheet is a valuable resource for anyone looking to sharpen their persuasive skills. It provides a structured approach to developing and organizing your persuasion strategies, making your arguments more compelling and your communication more impactful.

- **Bonus 2 - Gestures and Glances: A Daily Journal for Observing Body Language**

  This journal is an excellent tool for enhancing your nonverbal communication skills. It guides you in observing and interpreting body language, helping you gain deeper insights into the unspoken elements of communication, and improving your ability to respond effectively.

- **Bonus 3 - The Art of Expression: A Journey Through Communication Style Quizzes**

  Embark on a self-discovery journey to uncover your unique communication style. These quizzes are designed to help you understand and embrace your natural style of expression, and learn how to adapt it to various situations for more effective interactions.

- **Bonus 4 - Narrative Alchemy: Transforming Thoughts into Compelling Story Ideas**

  Unlock the power of storytelling with this creative guide. Whether you're a writer, a professional, or simply someone who loves to share stories, this resource will help you transform your thoughts and experiences into engaging and compelling narratives.

- **Bonus 5 - Words That Work: A Logbook for Successful Communication Strategies**

  This logbook is a practical tool for tracking and refining your communication strategies over time. By recording your experiences and observations, you'll be able to identify patterns, improve your approach, and develop more effective communication tactics.

How to Access Your Bonuses:

Scan the QR Code Below: Use your phone's camera or a QR code reader to scan the code for instant access to the bonus content.

SCAN ME

Or visit the Link: https://bit.ly/Weber-EC to access these resources.

I am confident that these bonuses will provide you with additional insight, practice, and reflection opportunities to further your mastery in the art of communication. Thank you for joining me on this enlightening journey.

Warm regards,

Emma Leigh Weber

Resources

Adler, R.B., Rodman, G., & Sévigny, A. (2017). Understanding human communication (13th ed.). Oxford University Press.

Beebe, S.A., Beebe, S.J., & Redmond, M.V. (2020). Interpersonal communication: Relating to others (9th ed.). Pearson.

Berko, R.M., Wolvin, A. D., & Wolvin, D. R. (2017). Communicating: A social and career focus (14th ed.). Houghton Mifflin.

Brooks, B.D., & Heath, R.L. (2021). Contemporary public speaking: How to craft and deliver a powerful speech (2nd ed.). Houghton Mifflin Harcourt.

Burgoon, J.K., Hunsaker, F.G., & Dawson, E.J. (2021). Human communication (6th ed.). SAGE Publications.

Coopman, S.J., & Lull, J. (2022). Public speaking: The evolving art (5th ed.). Cengage Learning.

Eunson, B. (2021). Communicating in the 21st century (5th ed.). John Wiley & Sons.

Fujishin, R. (2021). Creating effective groups: The art of small group communication (4th ed.). Rowman & Littlefield.

Grice, G.L., & Skinner J.F. (2019). Mastering public speaking (11th ed.). Pearson.

Gronbeck, B.E. (2021). Principles of speech communication (19th ed.). Routledge.

Holtgraves, T. (2020). Language as social action: Social psychology and language use. Routledge.

Ivy, D.K., & Backlund, P. (2018). GenderSpeak: Personal effectiveness in gender communication (6th ed.). Pearson.

Lucas, S.E. (2022). The art of public speaking (14th ed.). McGraw-Hill.

McCornack, S. (2018). Reflect & relate: An introduction to interpersonal communication (5th ed.). Bedford/St. Martin's.

Morreale, S., Spitzberg, B.H., & Barge, J.K. (2021). Human communication: Motivation, knowledge and skills (4th ed.). Routledge.

Nelson, P.E., & Pearson, J.C. (2021). Confidence in public speaking (11th ed.). McGraw-Hill.

Sollitto, M., Johnson, Z.D., & Myers, S.A. (2022). Communication that matters: How student voice perspectives inform pedagogy. Routledge.

Trenholm, S., & Jensen, A. (2021). Interpersonal communication (9th ed.). Oxford University Press.

Zarefsky, D. (2021). Public speaking: Strategies for success (9th ed.). Pearson.

Printed in Great Britain
by Amazon

41591721R00079